Consciousness and Moral Status

It seems obvious that phenomenally conscious experience is something of great value, and that this value maps onto a range of important ethical issues. For example, claims about the value of life for those in Permanent Vegetative State (PVS); debates about treatment and study of disorders of consciousness; controversies about end-of-life care for those with advanced dementia; and arguments about the moral status of embryos, fetuses, and non-human animals arguably turn on the moral significance of various facts about consciousness. However, though work has been done on the moral significance of elements of consciousness, such as pain and pleasure, little explicit attention has been devoted to the ethical significance of consciousness.

In this book Joshua Shepherd presents a systematic account of the value present within conscious experience. This account emphasizes not only the nature of consciousness, but also the importance of items within experience such as affect, valence, and the complex overall shape of particular valuable experiences. Shepherd also relates this account to difficult cases involving non-humans and humans with disorders of consciousness, arguing that the value of consciousness influences and partially explains the degree of moral status a being possesses, without fully determining it. The upshot is a deeper understanding of both the moral importance of phenomenal consciousness and its relations to moral status.

This book will be of great interest to philosophers and students of ethics, bioethics, philosophy of psychology, philosophy of mind, and cognitive science.

Joshua Shepherd is Assistant Professor in the Philosophy Department at Carleton University, Canada, and Research Professor at the University of Barcelona, Spain.

Routledge Focus on Philosophy

Routledge Focus on Philosophy is an exciting and innovative new series, capturing and disseminating some of the best and most exciting new research in philosophy in short book form. Peer reviewed and at a maximum of fifty thousand words shorter than the typical research monograph, *Routledge Focus on Philosophy* titles are available in both ebook and print-on-demand format. Tackling big topics in a digestible format, the series opens up important philosophical research for a wider audience, and as such is invaluable reading for the scholar, researcher, and student seeking to keep their finger on the pulse of the discipline. The series also reflects the growing interdisciplinarity within philosophy and will be of interest to those in related disciplines across the humanities and social sciences.

Available:

- **Plant Minds**, *Chauncey Maher*
- **The Logic of Commitment**, *Gary Chartier*
- **The Passing of Temporal Well-Being**, *Ben Bramble*
- **How We Understand Others**, *Shannon Spaulding*
- **Consciousness and Moral Status**, *Joshua Shepherd*

For more information about this series, please visit: www.routledge.com/philosophy/series/RFP

Consciousness and Moral Status

Joshua Shepherd

Routledge
Taylor & Francis Group
LONDON AND NEW YORK

First published 2018
by Routledge
2 Park Square, Milton Park, Abingdon, Oxon OX14 4RN

and by Routledge
605 Third Avenue, New York, NY 10017

First issued in paperback 2020

Routledge is an imprint of the Taylor & Francis Group, an informa business

British Library Cataloguing-in-Publication Data
A catalogue record for this book is available from the British Library

Library of Congress Cataloging-in-Publication Data
A catalog record for this book has been requested

ISBN 13: 978-0-367-73437-4 (pbk)
ISBN 13: 978-1-138-22161-1 (hbk)

Typeset in Times New Roman
by Apex CoVantage, LLC

For: Kelly, Zooey, and Finn
To: The Uehiro community, with much gratitude

Contents

Part I

Preliminaries

1 Introduction

Billy lay on a couch. His head throbbed. He had the chills. It hurt to stand. Outside was cold and gray. It started to rain. Billy looked towards his garden. A dog – Mrs. Ruffles, an old golden retriever – sat at the window, searching for his eyes. He made eye contact. Mrs. Ruffles began to whine.

He had forgotten about Mrs. Ruffles. He was keeping her for a friend. She was clearly miserable. Billy knew he should go let her in. A thought occurred to him. *Mrs. Ruffles is just a dog.* He felt terrible for thinking it. But he also felt ill enough to wonder whether he might just stay on the couch for a few moments more. The misery of Mrs. Ruffles was placed on the balance next to his.

He really ought to go let her in. I'm not trying to suggest otherwise. I just want to focus on his thought – *Mrs. Ruffles is just a dog.* It's a common thought. It contains an interesting suggestion. The suggestion is that there is some reason, something associated with the kind of thing Mrs. Ruffles is, and the kind of thing Billy is, for thinking that the misery of Mrs. Ruffles counts for less than Billy's. Maybe the suggestion is that her misery is somehow not as bad as Billy's. But what could that mean? Is that a defensible thought?

While we are comparing miseries, compare these two. First, the misery I might experience if I were to visit a Lobster Shack and decline to order the lobster. Second, the misery a lobster might experience if I ordered it. *It's just a lobster*. Right? The thing will get boiled alive. How bad is that for a lobster?

These cases occur all the time, to most of us. They are familiar. Some of the questions I want to ask in this book arise from such cases, and relate to a familiar kind of moral reflection regarding the nature of the good life, and the nature of right and wrong action. We lack consensus regarding answers to these questions. But we have spent a lot of time reflecting on them. That's not nothing. However, some of the questions I want to ask arise from less familiar cases. And some of these less familiar cases highlight practical and ethical questions facing advanced modern societies – questions about which we have spent much less time reflecting. As a result, our moral discourse surrounding such cases is less advanced, and moral consensus, even if possible, is probably further away.

Here is one such kind of case. In the near future, our technical skill at manipulating the genetic code is much advanced. For example, we are able to turn off a pig's genetic program for growing a kidney, to insert a human pluripotent stem cell into the embryo of a pig, and to bring a pig with a developing human kidney into the world. Moreover, we can do so in a way that generates an easily and safely transplantable kidney – provided we keep the pig in sterile conditions and 'sacrifice' it once the kidney has reached the right stage. Another thing we can do is this: we can use human stem cells to alter the developing nervous system of a range of animals. For example, mice are able to incorporate elements of the human nervous system – certain kinds of neurons and glial cells – and these mice demonstrate impressive gains on a range of cognitive tests. There are good scientific reasons for performing this procedure, of course. Doing so allows us to study the progress of developmental processes and of various kinds of infections, and to test certain kinds of psycho-active drugs, in animals that we do not mind killing. The results are highly valuable for understanding what goes wrong in the human nervous system and how we might develop fixes. Of course, the results might be even better if we altered the nervous systems of animals more similar to us – Great Apes, for example. Some scientists argue that, given the benefits, we ought to get over our moral misgivings and experiment on Great Apes. *They're just animals, after all.* Others argue that not only should we ban research on apes, but we should also ban it on mice. Some in this camp also argue that we should ban the use of pigs as organ hosts. Still others take an intermediate position: it is wrong to experiment on apes, but not necessarily on mice. And, given the benefits, it is okay to use pigs as hosts for human organs. Of course, a large part of the disagreement in all these cases stems from disagreements about the kind or amount of value present in the mental lives of all these different animals.

Here is a second kind of case. Hedda is a fun-loving mother of three and a devoted wife. While skiing in Italy, Hedda crashes into a tree and sustains a traumatic brain injury. After several days in coma, Hedda begins to show minimal signs of recovery. The doctors are initially pessimistic. The damage is severe. Nonetheless Hedda shows signs of awareness. In particular, she sometimes makes unintelligible sounds when her family is in the room. And she sometimes reacts to music. According to one of her nurses, she enjoys Johnny Cash, especially the older stuff. Hedda is assessed and diagnosed as being in Minimally Conscious State (MCS). This is a diagnosis that indicates a level of functional sophistication above that of the Vegetative State.

Even so, the doctors believe there is no chance of full recovery, and little chance of recovery beyond MCS. Hedda will never be able to communicate her wishes regarding her own care, nor will she be able to truly understand her own condition. After an initial period of grief, Hedda's family comes to believe that she would not want to continue living in this condition. They recall instances before the injury when Hedda seemed to indicate as much. Still, in the absence of clearly expressed prior wishes, the legal issues surrounding Hedda's case are complex. Her family will likely need to press the case in court if they want artificial nutrition and hydration removed. Although Hedda's husband was initially happy at the diagnosis of MCS, he comes to see this diagnosis as a burden. The reason is that if Hedda was diagnosed as in Vegetative State, they could probably have artificial nutrition and hydration removed without involving the legal system, and Hedda could have the death her husband judges she would want. Unlike her husband, one of Hedda's nurses is glad that Hedda was properly diagnosed. He knows that many patients who should be diagnosed as in MCS are misdiagnosed as Persistently Vegetative. And he thinks this is a tragedy – for vegetative patients rarely get a chance to receive proper care. But Hedda's nurse believes that with proper care, she can have a positive quality of life. *She is conscious, after all*, he thinks. *That's something we should respect.*

I'll mention one more kind of case here. It is the future. Your granddaughter turns out to be a brilliant engineer. One day she comes over for tea, and begins discussing a difficult case at her lab. Using highly advanced neuromorphic technology, she and her colleagues have developed a range of computer programs that approximate and sometimes far outpace the mental capacities of an adult human. Typically these programs are used in machines that do one thing very well – things like enable a self-driving car to perceive its environmental surroundings, or enable an autonomous weapons system to discriminate between a combatant and a non-combatant. But lately they have been experimenting with ways to put some of these disparate capacities together in a kind of robot. Your granddaughter describes the shocked reaction of many in the lab when one of these robots was going through a series of tests. Apparently after answering a range of questions designed to test its inferential capacities, the robot offered a question of its own. 'After these tests,' it said, 'is it your intention to turn me off?' After your granddaughter leaves, you pull a dusty book down off the shelf. It is an old philosophy of mind anthology, given to you (as you now recall) by your granddaughter after she took a philosophy course at university. The reason you are thumbing through the anthology is that now you are suddenly gripped by the thought that this robot in your granddaughter's lab might actually be conscious. *If that's true*, you think, *then is this thing more than just a robot?*

In spite of important differences in detail and in ancillary moral issues, at the heart of these cases are worries about the moral significance of consciousness. In particular, these cases highlight puzzlement about the kind of value that may be present in different kinds of conscious entities, and accordingly about the nature of our reasons to treat these entities in various ways. Let Mrs. Ruffles in? Eat the lobster? Give Hedda intensive medical care or allow her to die? Experiment on mice with partially human brains? Turn the robot off or begin to think of it as a person? My view on questions like these is that it is difficult to answer them without some understanding of the kind or kinds of value associated with the kind or kinds of conscious mentality involved.

Developing such an understanding is my aim in this book. I want to know about a certain kind of value that attaches to consciousness – why it attaches, how much of it might be there (and why), and what kinds of reasons for action might be related to the value within consciousness.

Fair warning: nothing like a moral algorithm, or even moral certainty regarding these cases, is forthcoming. These are difficult cases for a reason. The hope is by the end of the book, we will be able to see more clearly why these cases are so difficult, as well as what we are committing to when we commit to one or another course of action.

The first thing to do is to get as clear as possible regarding the central concepts in play: consciousness, value, and moral status. That is the task of the next three chapters.

Note

Research for this book was supported by the Wellcome Trust, Award 104347.

2 Preliminaries

Consciousness

Consciousness is polysemous. One way to get a sense of this is to read the entry for 'consciousness' in the *Oxford English Dictionary*. Six different definitions are discussed. It is tempting to spend the day mapping the relationships between them – do they all share some core of meaning, or not? – but I won't do that here. The point is to note that a wide range of legitimate uses of the term 'consciousness' will not be directly at issue in this book. For example, sometimes we use 'consciousness' to refer to a state of awareness or knowledge of something, whether internal or external: on a long bike ride, I can be conscious of my bodily sensations of elation, the contours of the trail in front of me, a hawk overhead, etc. Sometimes we use 'consciousness' with connotations of the self or the person. In this connection, the OED offers an interesting quote from Conder (1877, 91): 'From our innermost consciousness a voice is heard, clothed with native authority. I feel. I think. I will. I am.' Sometimes we are more reductive, using 'consciousness' to refer simply to the state of being awake. For example, we sometimes describe waking from a deep sleep as regaining consciousness.

The kind of consciousness at issue in this book is not *exactly* the ones just discussed (although they seem to me to need this kind of consciousness in certain ways). The kind at issue here is what philosophers and psychologists call 'phenomenal consciousness.' In the philosophy and science of consciousness we say that phenomenal consciousness is a feature or aspect of mental states, events, and processes. The feature or aspect is that *there is something it is like for you* to token or undergo these mental states, events, and processes.

That terminology is meant not to elucidate so much as point to phenomenal consciousness. Here is another way to point to it, drawing on some of the ways we use the word 'consciousness.' You wake from dreamless sleep, and it seems to you that you have regained consciousness. What did you regain? Speaking for myself, it seems I regain a kind of experiential field – a space populated by all sorts of mental states, events, and processes. In the normal case, this field will contain perceptual bits (visual states, olfactory states, auditory states), bits due to imagination (that song playing in my head), bits due to thought (worries about what I have to do today), bits due to attention (focus directed at a noise I hear, or at a pain in my back), and on and on. This space is a shifting, dynamic thing – it seems to change as the world around me and in me changes. So we sometimes speak of a stream of consciousness, and the way that the stream flows. This space also seems to connect me in a very intimate way with the world. So we sometimes speak of being conscious of various objects and events in the external world.

What it is like for me at some time is many things, then. It is all of that. And that is phenomenal consciousness.

Faced with the diversity present within the experiential field, one might hope the philosopher will have a way of carving up the field in some way – drawing illuminating distinctions, constructing taxonomies of various types of conscious experience, offering a way to get some grip on the architecture of this unwieldy phenomenon. I'll do my best to do some of this in what follows. For now, however, I wish to keep things as simple as possible. I am examining the thought that phenomenal consciousness is somehow valuable. So I will begin (in Chapter 5) by considering phenomenal consciousness as a whole. As we will see, we will have to move on to more detailed consideration of aspects of consciousness.

3 Preliminaries

Value

A guiding thought for this book is that phenomenal consciousness contains value. What does that mean? Let me begin indirectly, by focusing on the ways that we *place* value on things.

We place value on a wide range of things – on objects, on events, on states of affairs, on collections of objects or events or states of affairs. We do so in two closely related ways. First, we take up a range of valuing attitudes towards the things in question. Second, we behave towards these things in ways that reflect – and are usually explained by – these valuing attitudes. What valuing attitudes we take up will depend on how we evaluate the thing. Human evaluative practices are complex: just go to any on-line discussion forum regarding science fiction films or professional sports teams. Depending on the thing and on our evaluation of it, we might like it, love it, desire it, approve of it, respect it, stand in awe of it, feel guilt about it, be surprised by it, hate it, fear it, regret it, feel sadness over it, be interested in it, be annoyed or angry or disgusted by it, and more. How best to organize the space of valuing attitudes is an interesting and difficult question.

For example, some of these attitudes apply cleanly to items considered in abstraction from one's own circumstances. I might like or approve of an action performed by an agent who lived three thousand years ago, even though the action has no influence on me or my circumstances. Other attitudes are more naturally seen as evaluations of an item in relation to one's own circumstances. When I regret or fear something, it is usually because I stand in a particular, personally relevant relationship to it. Further, some evaluative attitudes obviously reflect positive or negative evaluations (e.g., love, hate), while the valence of other attitudes is not immediately clear. Does awe reflect a positive or negative evaluation, some mix of the two, or neither? It is hard to say (see McShane 2013). Note that there is no good reason to think the things on which we place value must be easily classified as good or bad. We often offer mixed evaluations of things – something can be an item of love, desire, fear, awe, interest, and disgust. Facts about the value of a thing will often resist answers in terms of simple scales and simple dichotomies.

So it turns out that placing value on things is a fairly normal, yet fairly complex, part of human life. We can regiment the complexity somewhat by invoking a distinction between derivative and non-derivative value. It is non-derivative value that is the fundamental notion. As a gloss on it, people often say that a thing has non-derivative value if it has (or bears) value in itself, on its own, or in its own right. By contrast, a thing has derivative value in virtue of some connection it bears to things with non-derivative value. Often the connection is elucidated in terms of a thing's usefulness. The taste of fried okra is extremely good, and it is plausible to think that whatever your list of items that bear non-derivative value, extremely good taste experiences will be on it. Such experiences have value in their own right. Now you can't make good fried okra without a decent fryer. So a fryer is a thing with derivative value in the sense that it is useful for getting you to a thing with non-derivative value: the experience of eating fried okra. Short of a pretty good argument to convince us otherwise, it looks like a mistake to place non-derivative value on a good fryer (where good means good at frying, not good in its own right), or to place merely derivative value on the experience of eating fried okra.

I have been talking about the ways that we place value on things. This book is not, however, about how we place value. This book is about the value that things – in particular, conscious experiences – have. To get a feel for that distinction, think about what you think when one of your friends fails to see the value you see in something (a great movie, a great meal, a lovely person, etc.). You think that they are, for some reason, *missing what is there*. There's value there, you think, it's obvious, and your friend misses it.

In this book, then, I'm going to be interested in the non-derivative value present within consciousness. In reflecting on this, I will be trying to account not only for the value that is present in consciousness, but also to understand what makes the items that bear value bear the value that they do. I want to know not only what things within consciousness have non-derivative value: I want to know why they have that value.

We are still in the preliminary phases. But I need to say a little more about non-derivative value. As I understand it, non-derivative value is a general or determinable category containing sub-types. One potential sub-type is intrinsic value. This is value an entity bears in virtue of its intrinsic properties (if you believe in intrinsic properties).[1] Another potential sub-type is essential value. This is value an entity bears in virtue of its essential properties – the properties that make it what it is (see Rønnow-Rasmussen 2011, Chapter 1, for some discussion). Christine Korsgaard (1983) and others (Rabinowicz and Rønnow-Rasmussen 2000) have argued for existence of a further sub-type. They argue that entities can bear non-derivative value not in virtue of intrinsic or essential properties, but in virtue of their relations to external entities. Korsgaard thinks this is the kind of value a beautiful painting bears. If locked up permanently in a closet, the painting is of no value. But under the condition that it can be (or is) viewed, the painting is valuable. So its value is not just a matter of its intrinsic or essential properties. But neither is its value simply a function of its usefulness in generating valuable aesthetic experiences. The painting is valuable in its own right – non-derivatively – when it stands in a certain relationship to viewers. As Korsgaard puts it,

> [A]lthough its value is not intrinsic, the painting may be objectively good for its own sake. If it were viewed, and the viewer were enraptured, or satisfied, or instructed by its loveliness, then the painting would be an objectively good thing: for the world would be, really, a better place for it: it would be a substantive contribution to the actual sum of goodness of the world.
>
> (1983, 186)

I am not here endorsing everything Korsgaard is saying. I am illustrating that things may bear more than one kind of non-derivative value. This might be thought to complicate our inquiry. Perhaps some items within consciousness are intrinsically valuable, perhaps some are essentially valuable, and so on. Perhaps some items have value in their own right provided they stand in certain relations to other things. In Chapter 8 we will look at an argument by G.E. Moore that comes close to this kind of view. According to Moore, experiences may be of little value on their own, but may be a part of a very valuable whole if the experiences provide the right kind of connection between conscious subjects and items in the world that have great value.

I think our inquiry *might* involve wrinkles due to different kinds of non-derivative value. But in this book I am going to focus on what I take to be the core of the non-derivative value present within consciousness. In my view, this will be a kind of essential value, insofar as it will be a value that obtains in virtue of the relevant items' essential properties.[2]

One final point is worth mentioning at this preliminary stage. It will arise again. Notice that in characterizing our value-placing activities, I noted the wide range of ways we might take up valuing attitudes and valuing behaviors. The very existence of this diversity suggests that at some level value has a kind of shape. What I mean by this is that different kinds of entities may bear value, including non-derivative value, in different ways. Whether this is due to differences in the descriptive features of the things that bear value, or due to differences in their normative properties – e.g., the kind of value they bear or the kind of good-makers or bad-makers they exemplify – is not something I will comment on right here. What I wish to mention at this preliminary stage is simply that it makes sense to think that the complexity of our valuing practices reflects a complexity in the ways things bear value, such that the valuing attitudes and behaviors called for by various valuable things *should* reflect this complexity. Put differently, the way some entity bears non-derivative value will generate particular reasons to token particular valuing attitudes and to engage in particular patterns of action. Marcia Baron articulates something much like this idea in the following passage.

> Value comes in many varieties . . . and it doesn't appear that all value calls for the same response. Some are such that the best response is to exemplify or instantiate them; still others call for producing as much of them as possible; others call for honoring them by refraining from doing anything that would violate them. A mixture of these responses will often be called for, a mixture whose proper proportions may differ, depending on the value and the particular situation.
>
> (Baron, in Baron, Pettit, and Slote 1997, 22)

I mention this early on because it is important to avoid the kind of moral philosophy that reduces reflection on value and valuing practices to a simple contest between amounts of value and injunctions to maximize simply construed amounts. One aim in this book is to assist our thinking regarding difficult problem cases. If facts about value are of the wrong sort to be captured by talk of amounts of value, it is of no help to offer up formulas regarding amounts, and to advise attitudes and action in service of the greater amounts. This is not, of course, to say that reflection on amounts of value will be of no use. Sometimes we can see clearly a difference between amounts of value. But in many of the problem cases, we cannot. And it may be that our problem is not simply epistemic.

As I will emphasize later, it may be important to pay attention not only to the amount of value a thing might bear, but to way that it bears it. This latter feature may give rise to reasons for valuing attitudes and patterns of action not explicable by a reductive calculus of amounts.

Notes

1 What intrinsic properties are is a controversial matter, but one way to think of it is in terms of duplication: if you were travelling in space, and you found a perfect duplicate of some earth-bound entity on a different planet, the intrinsic properties of that entity on earth would necessarily be present in the extra-terrestrial entity as well (and vice versa, of course).

2 Why not the items' intrinsic properties? Although the two notions are logically distinct, I am not sure the distinction matters much for present purposes. On some views of consciousness, however, the presence of certain external objects is essential to the nature of some conscious experiences (see, e.g., Fish 2008). It would be strange, however, to say that the presence of certain external objects is intrinsic to the nature of these experiences. To remain neutral regarding such a view, I speak only of essential properties.

4 Preliminaries

Moral status

The notion of moral status has come to occupy a central role in the practical ethics literature. The fundamental idea underlying the notion of moral status is given by Mary Anne Warren in the following passage.

> To have moral status is to be morally considerable, or to have moral standing. It is to be an entity toward which moral agents have, or can have, moral obligations. If an entity has moral status, then we may not treat it in just any way we please.
>
> (1997, 3)

Now, there may be moral obligations to entities that are derived in an indirect way. I might have an obligation not to desecrate some object you regard as sacred. This does not entail that the object has moral status – my obligation regarding the object may obtain in virtue of my obligations to you (see Harman 2007). So we should add some qualifier, according to which an entity has moral status only if it *itself* matters morally, or, as Jaworska and Tennenbaum (2013) put it, only if it matters morally *for the entity's own sake*. I will put this qualifier as follows: an entity's moral status is a function of its nature.

This much leaves it entirely open what kinds of entities might have moral status. This is to the good, for it is arguable that biological entities of many sorts, as well as features of the natural environment (e.g., ecosystems, rivers, mountains) and even important artifacts (e.g., works of art or items of great historical significance) have moral status. This much also leaves it entirely open why an entity may have moral status. And this is to the good as well, for this is a substantive ethical issue, not to be settled by fiat.

This latter point has been made by others (e.g., Rachels 2004; DeGrazia 2008; Sachs 2011). It is important enough to underline. An attribution of moral status to an entity is, as David DeGrazia has said, a 'convenient shorthand for general assertions about our moral obligations to beings of different sorts and the grounds of those obligations' (2008, 184). Moral status is not an independent factor that secures monolithic treatment for all who have it. It is a kind of placeholder for attribution of reasons to regard and treat an entity in certain ways. An attribution of moral status does not tell us what these reasons are, nor does it tell us why they exist. To determine this, we need a more substantive account of the reasons we have to regard and treat an entity in certain ways, and an account of the grounds of these reasons.

What, then, are those grounds of our obligations to an entity that hold in virtue of its nature? It has to be said that much of the current literature on moral status is not well placed to provide an answer to this question. This is because much (although not all) of the current literature builds in an assumption regarding moral status. The assumption is that adult human beings are the paradigm case of an entity with moral status. Sometimes this assumption is fleshed out further by the claim that adult human beings have full moral status – a term that at least implies that moral status is what some call a threshold concept. That is, although moral status comes in amounts, there is a place beyond which moral status ceases to increase. If we think that healthy human adults are exemplars of moral status, it is natural to think that at least they will occupy this place of full moral status.

I can understand why many proceed under this assumption. It captures an element of commonsense morality, according to which human beings are in some sense worth more than non-humans. And it seems epistemically modest, in the sense that it allows us to move from something we seem to be in a decent position to know, namely the grounds of the moral status of adult human beings, to elements that are more difficult to know, namely the grounds of whatever moral status other beings have. Conceiving of things in this way generates talk of the 'ethics of marginal cases,' which is constituted by consideration of the moral status of entities that depart from the paradigm in various ways and that thus qualify as potentially marginal with respect to their moral status.

As I say, this is understandable. But it is pernicious. One reason is that it sets the theorist off on an unguided quest to discover the grounds of healthy adult human moral status, armed only with the intuition that it exists. But it turns out that this quest generates as little agreement as many other philosophical quests. Adult humans are complicated creatures, with a range of potentially morally relevant capacities and properties. Theorists have variously seized on many of these to offer accounts of the grounds of moral status. These include possession of self-consciousness (Tooley 1972), possession of sophisticated psychological capacities (McMahan 2002), possession of 'typical human capacities' (DiSilvestro 2010), possession of the capacity to participate in a 'person-rearing relationship' (Jaworska and

Tennenbaum 2014), possession of a capacity for intentional agency (Sebo 2017), the ability to take oneself to be an end rather than a mere means in the sense that one can experience and pursue what is good for one (Korsgaard 2013), the capacity to suffer (Bentham 1996), possession of the genetic basis for moral agency (Liao 2010), and no doubt more. Of course some of these are friendlier to entities outside the tight circle of healthy adult humans, and some are not. What is striking, however, about many of these accounts is that they do not seek to justify the assumption that healthy adult humans are the paradigm case. Rather, this assumption justifies their search for the features in virtue of which the assumption must be true. But if healthy adult humans are not the paradigm case, the search may be headed in the wrong direction from the get go.

If so, a further difficulty arises. To see how, consider the primary motivation for developing an account of the grounds of moral status under the assumption that healthy adult humans are the paradigm case. The motivation is to figure out a way to *extend* moral status to the marginal cases, and to do so in a way that respects theoretical constraints peculiar to the cases at issue. The procedure is thus to find some features in common between cases, or, failing that, to connect the cases via philosophical ingenuity. But thus described, the procedure runs the risk of skipping the crucial first step, namely, the elucidation and justification of the grounds for moral status assumed to apply to healthy adult humans. In this dialectical context, it can seem meritorious for one's argument to demonstrate a way to connect the paradigm with the marginal case. But of course that is only so if the entire theoretical structure is in good standing – if one actually has a good account of the grounds of moral status. There may be many ways to connect features of adult humans with marginal cases. What we should ask is not whether they can be connected, but whether the grounds of moral status attributed to adult humans are compelling in the first place, and whether the moral status of a marginal case ought to depend on the theoretical connection to an adult human in any case.

Rather than focus overmuch on the human case, I propose a more abstract, but workable, understanding of moral status. It includes two ideas. First, if an entity has moral status, it does in virtue of its nature (i.e., of its essential properties) – of the properties that make that entity what it is. Second, not just any feature of an entity's nature is relevant. The features that are relevant will be those features in virtue of which the entity possesses, or bears, non-derivative value.

Moral status

An entity E bears moral status if and only if E bears non-derivative value. Moreover, the particular reasons we have to treat E in various ways are largely a function of way E bears whatever non-derivative value she does.[1,2]

This proposal leaves it open whether we should think of moral status as a threshold concept or not. It also leaves it open whether moral status comes in degrees, and if so, how we ought to understand the nature of the relevant scale(s). This is as it should be, for those kinds of claims should not be derived from the meaning of moral status. Moral status is a term of art, deployed by moral theorists. These more substantive issues should be settled by appeal to one's more substantive theory of non-derivative value and the ways entities bear non-derivative value.

Notes

1 Entities can bear both derivative and non-derivative value, and both can generate reasons to treat the entity in various ways. But the non-derivative value will in general trump the derivative value, unless it is connected to an usually powerful source of non-derivative value in some way. (So, for example, it is generally wrong to kill a human being. But if that human being is useful in that her death will save one billion other humans, the general injunction against killing may be overcome.)

2 Combining this claim with the view I develop next, on which conscious experiences bear value, might be thought to generate awkwardness. Am I suggesting that conscious experiences have fundamental moral status, and conscious subjects have moral status only derivatively? No. First, I leave it open that there are other ways beyond consciousness that a conscious subject could bear non-derivative value. But more importantly, I would think the plausible way to construe matters here is to say that talk of conscious experiences is elliptical for talk of a conscious subject tokening an experience, and that talk of an experience bearing value is elliptical for talk of the way that conscious subjects bear value.

Part II

An account of phenomenal value

5 What it is like and beyond

> [T]he marvel of consciousness – that sudden window swinging open on a sunlit landscape amidst the night of non-being.
>
> (Vladimir Nabokov)

Sometimes I find myself unhappily contemplating my own death. I figure after I'm dead I won't be too bothered about it. But dying still seems to represent some significant losses. What is it I don't want to lose? I want to say that one of the things I don't want to lose – and here I'm demonstrating with some kind of internal pointer – is: *this*. I look out my window, at the sunlight on the backside of Pembroke College's chapel. There's an old tree in the little yard behind it. It hasn't got its leaves back yet, though it has some bright red berries. I can hear the sounds of cars and pedestrians in the street below. I turn around in my chair. My trusty office mate Hannah looks up from her laptop, in my direction. I take a breath. I don't want to lose all of this. The world and my friends and my body and mind and the consciousness that seems so central to the way these things populate my life.

The goal here is not to understand the value of all these items as they are in the world. Rather, I wish to understand the value present within the phenomenal consciousness that is central to the way these things populate my life. Charles Siewert (1998) has attempted something similar – his work provides a nice entry point into some of the relevant issues (see also Kahane and Savulescu 2009).

Siewert proposes various versions of an interesting thought experiment. It involves conceiving of one's own mental life as lacking a certain feature – that of phenomenal consciousness. Siewert calls this procedure alternatively 'phenol-ectomy,' or 'zombification':

> Suppose you thought you faced the choice between (a) continuing on leading the sort of phenomenally conscious life you expect to live, or (b) undergoing a radical phenol-ectomy, which will make you permanently

> unable to have conscious experience, but will leave you (or your body) in possession of those features, for which sake you ordinarily value possession of phenomenal features: thus the nonphenomenal benefits will be the same on either option. And suppose you set aside any concerns having to do with the risks that the procedure may not work as planned. Then, if you still prefer the retention of at least *some* of them (you think (a) – the consciousness plan – is better than (b) – zombification), you do value having phenomenal features for its own sake. On the other hand, if you find that you would be *indifferent* to (or even *prefer*) the total loss of consciousness, when convinced that this would lose you none of the nonphenomenal benefits you assume would come with consciousness, then you find that you do not value consciousness for its own sake after all. (320)

What is lost when one undergoes phenol-ectomy? Arguably, one might token a wide range of mental states and undergo a wide range of mental episodes without phenomenal consciousness. I say 'arguably' because, at present, it is *de rigueur* in the philosophy and sciences of the mind to think that non-conscious mental processes are (both conceivably and actually) sophisticated, and indeed capable of performing many (if not all) of the functions we might attribute to conscious processes, without the aid of consciousness. This may turn out to be not quite right, or even terribly mistaken, but I'm following custom here in assuming this. On this assumption, then, after phenol-ectomy one might still desire things, believe things, intend things, fear things, hope things, undergo emotional reactions to events, make plans for the future, judge that brie is better than cheddar, and so on. Devoid of phenomenal consciousness, however, there would be nothing it is like to token such mental states and undergo such mental episodes.

Siewert uses this thought experiment to reinforce a fairly simple intuition: 'I think most of us will agree that we think it better that there are ways it seems to us to have the experience we do on some occasions, than that such experiences are then missing' (310). The point of the thought experiment is to isolate phenomenal consciousness from any of the nonphenomenal benefits that phenomenal consciousness might be thought to provide. Once we make the isolation transparent, Siewert thinks our judgment about the case indicates that we intrinsically value phenomenal consciousness – we value it for its own sake. This is because our judgment is to prefer a life with phenomenal consciousness to a life devoid of it.

I think Siewert is right about 'our judgment,' if by this we mean the judgment a fairly strong majority of people would share. Some people might deny the thought experiment makes sense. But I suspect many would accept the experiment, and would judge in the way Siewert does, opting 'without hesitation' (321) for a life with consciousness as opposed to a life without.

Even so, questions linger. What about phenomenal consciousness renders it so seemingly valuable? Siewert is less clear on this point, though he does discuss a wide range of experience-types – sexual experiences, taste experiences, visual experiences of vivid color (as opposed to seeing in black and white), cognitive experiences of thought or of working out a math problem, and more. Faced with such an array, Siewert suggests along the way that although perhaps not everyone would value all of these experience-types, almost all of us will find something intrinsically valuable in at least some of them: 'you do value *sometimes* having *some* phenomenal features' (310).

Stated like that, Siewert is right. But his lack of specificity regarding the phenomenal features undergirding the value we place on the experiences opens him to at least three lines of attack.

The first line of attack asks whether we can sustain the claim that consciousness is in some way non-derivatively valuable once we keep in mind that the process of zombification removes nothing of functional significance. Neil Levy pursues this line in a recent paper, focusing on arenas of experience that seem closely connected to value in some way or another. For example, Levy considers the view that zombification would remove aesthetic experience – a sure and significant loss. But Levy is not convinced.

> I think that it is actually far from obvious that aesthetic experience is even partially inaccessible to my zombie twin. Because he is my functional twin, he has some kind of grasp of colour and timbre; since I *respond* to these features of the world, so does he.
>
> (2014, 134)

Levy runs a similar argument concerning a range of experiences: those related to desire satisfaction, those related to valuing features of the world, and the experience of pleasure and pain. Regarding such experiences, Levy claims that once we recognize that our zombie twin loses nothing of functional significance, the force of Siewert's thought experiment diminishes.

> Siewert compares the loss of phenomenal consciousness to the loss of colour vision; it is akin to moving from a coloured world to a black-and-white world. Perhaps the comparison is an apt one, but it is *very* hard to be sure. We don't lose colour vision when we lose phenomenal consciousness. Nor do we lose the ability to experience pleasure and pain, emotions, or sounds. We lose the ability to experience these

> things *phenomenally*, but to what extent that is a significant loss is very hard to judge.
>
> (135)

Levy is not denying that phenomenal consciousness has some non-derivative value. He is questioning the importance of what value it has. One way to read his argument, then, is as a request for more theory. If we wish to resist Levy's claims that much (or all) of what seems valuable about phenomenal consciousness can in fact be attributed to the functionality we (rightly or wrongly) associate with phenomenal consciousness, we need an account of what is valuable in phenomenal consciousness that goes beyond Siewert's thought experiment.

The second line of attack involves questioning the cogency of the thought experiment. According to some philosophers, zombies – beings functionally equivalent to us but lacking consciousness – are impossible to conceive. Among those who find zombies conceivable, many report finding the exercise difficult to perform. Can we really base an account of the value of phenomenal consciousness on such a thought experiment?

No doubt some will argue we can. But, given that the account I offer next makes no appeal to zombies, I do not wish to press this point here. In my view, Siewert's thought experiment is interesting, and should motivate further consideration of the issues at hand. Why is it that so many of us find the prospect of zombification chilling – indeed, as bad as death? This kind of reaction suggests that there is something about phenomenal consciousness that we highly value, even if we cannot conceive of phenomenal consciousness as fully separate from functional features. The proper response to this line of attack is, again, simply to offer a fuller account of what is valuable in phenomenal consciousness.

A third line of attack stems from an elaboration upon Siewert's position. One way to expand his account is to claim that what's valuable in phenomenal consciousness is simply the fact that there is something it is like to be in a conscious state, or to have a conscious episode. On this elaborated position, then, phenomenal consciousness is valuable solely in virtue of the property that attaches to all phenomenally conscious experiences – the property of 'what-it-is-like-ness.'

I don't know whether Siewert would endorse this view, although I doubt it: the view is pretty clearly false. If phenomenal consciousness is solely valuable in virtue of what-it-is-like-ness, we have no way to explain the difference between valuable and disvaluable experiences. Perhaps, then, we should say that phenomenal consciousness is valuable in part in virtue of what-it-is-like-ness, plus additional properties. What properties? On a natural way of thinking of the structure of phenomenal consciousness, what-it-is-like-ness is the most determinable phenomenal property (see Kriegel 2015). All others are more determinate. That is, all the manifold ways consciousness can be – think of visual experience, auditory experience, emotional experience, and so on – will represent more determinate ways for there to be something it is like. Siewert's examples of what is valuable within consciousness all involve more determinate phenomenal properties. So a part of our task here is to locate the more determinate phenomenal properties in virtue of which phenomenal consciousness possesses non-derivative value.

6 Evaluative phenomenal properties

> Wherever a process of life communicates an eagerness to him who lives it, there the life becomes genuinely significant. Sometimes the eagerness is more knit up with the motor activities, sometimes with the perceptions, sometimes with the imagination, sometimes with reflective thought. But, wherever it is found, there is the zest, the tingle, the excitement of reality; and there is 'importance' in the only real and positive sense in which importance ever anywhere can be.
>
> (William James)

The following claim is an important first step towards the account I'm going to offer.

> [Evaluative Claim] It is necessary and sufficient for the presence of some (non-derivative) value in a conscious experience that the experience has evaluative phenomenal properties.

This claim leaves open a few important issues that I will discuss in due course. First, it leaves open the possibility that additional features of phenomenal consciousness have or contribute to the non-derivative value of an experience. Second, it leaves open how we are to understand the amount – and perhaps the different kinds – of value present in an experience. The aim of [Evaluative Claim] is to specify the *core* of the non-derivative value present within phenomenal consciousness.

Importantly, [Evaluative Claim] leaves open exactly what evaluative phenomenal properties are. Now, some account of evaluative phenomenal properties is called for. But it has to be pitched at the right level of abstraction. The reason – as philosophers who work on different forms of affective, hedonic, emotional, or evaluative phenomenology will immediately grasp – is that the more fine-grained an account of evaluative phenomenal properties one offers, the more likely one is to meet with disagreement. There is little consensus regarding issues in this region.

Let us begin as simply as possible, with this notion of phenomenal properties. Phenomenal properties are the constituents of phenomenal character. Phenomenal character qualifies the particular way in which it is like something to have a particular experience. I hear the first moment of the song 'Long Road' by the band Pearl Jam; I feel a surge of emotions, including a kind of plaintive calm induced by the song's tempo, a gut-located thrill at hearing the song for the first time in a long time, the pleasure associated with good music, and more; I feel nostalgia associated with the mental imagery of being at a concert in New Orleans a long time ago; I have auditory imagery in line with my expectations regarding how the song will go. All of these elements of my experience have phenomenal properties – properties more precisely described as auditory (hearing the first notes), emotional (nostalgia and etc.), imagistic (I mentioned both visual and auditory imagery), and so on. All these phenomenal properties determine my experience's phenomenal character, which is a way of saying that all these phenomenal properties combine to give my experience the character it has.

Note, incidentally, that talk of properties can be flexible. We need not think of experiences as pointillist paintings. Some properties relevant to determining phenomenal character may specify relations between properties. In other words, there is something it is like to feel a gut-located thrill, and there is something it is like to hear the first moment of 'Long Road,' and there is something it is like to experience these two things *conjointly* (see Bayne 2010) (or in rapid succession within the specious present).

Like many of our experiences, the one I just described included evaluative properties. Indeed, it included a wide range of them. Perhaps the easiest to describe and to fit within a theory of value was the property of pleasure. Pleasure is a paradigmatically *valenced* evaluative property, in the sense that pleasure is – if not always, at least nearly so – a *positive* evaluative feature of experience. Other evaluative properties are somewhat more complex. Nostalgia is probably a rich complex of evaluative properties directed in a certain way – at some element of the past or some element associated with the past. I won't try to give an analysis of nostalgia, but it certainly looks to have a kind of mixed valence – it is in ways good and bad, and it's not even clear that its badness is all that bad.[1] The strong yearning one feels during some episodes of nostalgia may just be good in part because of way the melancholic, painful aspects combine in some way with other aspects attached to the experience.

I take it, then, that evaluative phenomenal properties are a common feature of most of our ongoing conscious experiences. But can we be a bit more perspicacious about the claim that these properties are *evaluative*?

In virtue of what? Allow me to try a clean, well-lighted answer. Evaluative phenomenal properties are evaluative in virtue of the fact that evaluation of some item – where item is broadly construed to include some other property, some object, event, state of affairs, relation, proposition, or whatever – is embedded in the relevant phenomenal character. Evaluative phenomenal properties qualify items via some form of evaluation, and their phenomenal character is an essential part of the way that they do so.

Even if correct, this explication of evaluative properties is too general to capture the kind of properties essential for non-derivative value. Consider the claim that consciously made judgments qualify items via a form of evaluation, and their proprietarily cognitive phenomenal character is an essential part of the way that they do so. I might think an evaluative thought like *this British IPA is flat and tastes nothing like a real IPA*, and the thought's status as an evaluative state or event (as opposed, perhaps, to a passing thought I do not endorse or find compelling) may depend on the cognitive phenomenal character of that thought (for discussion of cognitive phenomenal character, see Pitt 2004). The problem is that even if that is true, the cognitive phenomenology of that kind of thought is not the kind of thing that is necessary and sufficient for some non-derivative value. What is missing? In my view, what is missing is the presence of *affective* phenomenal properties. Since this is what I think, I have to offer a slightly more specific account of the relevant kind of evaluative phenomenal properties.

Affective phenomenal properties are phenomenal properties essential to affective experience: that is, hedonic experiences (involving pleasure and pain) and emotional experiences (involving the emotions, including so-called epistemic and so-called metacognitive emotions). Affective phenomenal properties are those responsible for the phenomenal character of painfulness present in an experience of a stubbed toe, the sinking character of sadness in an experience of grief, the quick thrilling burst present in the falling experience that comes with cliff jumping.

Exactly how affective properties figure in evaluative experiences quite generally is a matter of controversy. There are a number of competing accounts of the painfulness of pain, and of the pleasantness of pleasure. The same is true of accounts of the nature of emotions and emotional experience. I have my own preferences regarding these accounts, but I do not wish to commit to any one of them here. What I need to do is offer a sufficiently general account of the way affect figures in evaluative experience, one that makes as few enemies as possible and makes the claim I want to defend as plausible as possible.

Towards that end, let us consider different accounts of emotion and emotional experience. On the perceptual theory that Christine Tappolet defends, emotions are 'perceptual experiences of evaluative properties' (2016, 15). More specifically, emotions essentially involve perceptual experiences as of evaluative properties attributed to items, where the resultant experiences have non-conceptual content. Tappolet elaborates:

> Although emotions can, and often do, involve conceptually articulated contents – it is for instance clearly necessary to possess the concept of financial meltdown to experience fear that there will be a financial meltdown – the evaluative appraisal that is part of the content of emotions is non-conceptual. In other words, it is not necessary to possess the concept of the fearsome to experience fear and thereby to represent something as fearsome.
>
> (18)

If one adopts a perceptual theory of emotions, it is easy to see that affective properties will be essential to emotional experience, and also to see that affective properties will be essential to whether the experiences qualify as evaluative as well as to the way that they do. This is because on a perceptual theory the affective properties possess evaluative content. It is in virtue of affective properties that emotional experience is evaluative experience.

Of course, a perceptual theory makes specific commitments regarding the content of perceptual experience, and regarding the ability of affective properties to represent the range of things it seems our emotional experiences represent. One might worry that affective properties alone cannot do the required work (see Dokic and Lemaire 2013; Schroeter, Schroeter, and Jones 2015). And such a worry might lead one towards a non-perceptual account of emotional experience.

Julien Deonna and Fabrice Teroni (2011, 2015) defend a different view. On their Attitudinal Theory of emotion and emotional experience, emotions do not have evaluative contents. Rather, their phenomenology and their correctness conditions stem from their nature as evaluative attitudes. To appreciate the attitude/content distinction, note that it is possible to take several attitudes to the exact same content. If distinct emotions are distinct attitudes, one might take an attitude of fear, disgust, love, hate, or whatever to the content *that is a big dog*. How exactly would one do so? Deonna and Teroni argue that we do so via affective bodily phenomenology.

> [W]hat it is like to undergo bodily changes that occur in emotions is best glossed by saying that the subject feels herself taking a certain stance, posture or indeed attitude towards something outside her body. To put it differently, the idea is that, when undergoing an emotion, the body is felt globally or holistically as taking a certain attitude towards this or that object or event.
>
> (2015, 302)

How is it that bodily phenomenology can be seen as taking up an evaluative attitude? Deonna and Teroni assert that the kind of action-readiness that accompanies much emotional phenomenology somehow embeds an evaluation:

> Fear of a dog is an experience of the dog as dangerous insofar as it is an experience of one's body being prepared to forestall its impact . . . an attitude it is correct to have if, and only if, the dog is dangerous.
>
> (303)[2]

Regarding this proposal, however, one might worry that Deonna and Teroni are conflating correctness conditions with satisfaction conditions. If the attitude prepares one to forestall impact, the attitude will be satisfied if impact is forestalled – the attitude itself need not have anything to do with whether the dog is dangerous.

Indeed, one might go on to argue that the relevant bodily affective properties do not amount to anything properly construed as evaluative (see Dokic and Lemaire 2015 for a further elaboration on this line of thought). Rather, perhaps affective properties simply prepare us for action (including mental action) in various ways (Frijda 1987), and perhaps the evaluative nature of prototypical emotional experience is a matter of its being a complex combination of cognitive responses to and associations with affective phenomenology. It is, after all, common currency in the emotion literature that emotional experiences are often complex, and thus that picking out what is essential to emotions is a real chore. Tappolet articulates this nicely in discussing fear.

> You are strolling down a lonely mountain lane when suddenly a huge dog leaps towards you. Intense fear overcomes you. A number of different interconnected elements are involved here. First, there is the visual and auditory perception of the animal and its movements. In addition, it is likely that, however implicitly and inarticulately, you appraise the situation as acutely threatening. Then, there are a number of physiological changes, involving different systems controlled by the autonomic nervous system. Your heart is pounding, your breathing becomes strained, and you start trembling. These changes are accompanied by an expression of fear on your face: your mouth opens and your eyes widen as you stare at the dog. You also undergo a kind of experience, such as the feeling of a pang. Moreover, a number of thoughts are likely to cross your mind. You might think you'll never escape and that the dog is about to tear you to pieces. In addition, your attention focuses on the animal and its movements, as well as, possibly, on ways of escaping

> or of defending yourself. Accordingly, your fear is likely to come with a motivation, such as an urge to run away or to strike back.
>
> (2016, 7–8)

All of these elements – sensory experience, forms of appraisal, physiological changes, cognitive and attentional accompaniments, forms of action-readiness – are a part of a *paradigmatic* and evolutionarily ancient emotional experience (although our experiences of fear may have more or different components from those of our non-human ancestors and cousins). What is the upshot? My point in the foregoing, and in citing the long passage from Tappolet, has been to illustrate just how difficult it will be to develop a fine-grained account of the constitution of evaluative experience. Given the complexity present in paradigm emotional experiences, it is plausible that core types of evaluative experience will not be characterizable in terms of affective properties alone.

As I said earlier, my aim here is to offer a sufficiently general account of the way affect figures in evaluative experience, one that makes as few enemies as possible and makes the claim I want to defend as plausible as possible. I suggest this can be done by decomposing [Evaluative Claim] into the following two claims.

> [Affective Claim] It is necessary for the presence of some (non-derivative) value in a conscious experience that the experience has affective phenomenal properties.

> [Evaluative Claim] It is sufficient for the presence of some (non-derivative) value in a conscious experience that the experience has evaluative phenomenal properties that essentially contain affective phenomenal properties.

These claims are strictly neutral between perceptual, attitudinal, and other accounts of emotions and hedonic experiences, as well as various accounts of the role of affective properties in such experiences. So they are neutral on the important question of whether affective properties represent evaluative properties or not.

We can combine these two claims.

> [Affective-Evaluative Claim] It is necessary and sufficient for the presence of some (non-derivative) value in a conscious experience that the experience has evaluative phenomenal properties that essentially contain affective phenomenal properties.

In defense of this claim, consider these cases.

Depressed aesthete

Koharu is an expert wine taster, with an extremely subtle palate. When she started drinking wine, she loved it for its complexity, and she enjoyed exercising her considerable abilities in recognizing and describing the features of wines. Lately, however, she has been suffering from flat affect. She finds that she is still able to recognize and describe wines to a high level of accuracy. She can tell whether a wine is a thing of exquisite quality and sophistication, or whether it suffers in all the many ways wines can suffer. But there is no joy in her doing so. Indeed, in a way she notices, her experience of tasting wine is totally devoid of the rich evaluative properties that used to characterize this kind of experience. In trying to describe the experience to a friend, Koharu put it like this. 'I recognize that this is an excellent wine,' she said. 'It's not that I dislike the taste. But I don't like it either. It's just that there's nothing good about it.'

Weeping tourist

Saanvi visits London for the first time. She is a fan of art in the vague way that many of us are: she finds some art enjoyable to view, some art mystifying, and some boring. She doesn't have a great sense of why she likes what she likes – she's never really thought much about it. Saanvi visits the Tate Modern, and wanders into a large dim room full of large Rothko paintings. Something about the light in the room, and the colors and shapes in the paintings, moves Saanvi deeply. It is an unusual experience. But powerful. Without a thought about why, and without worrying about what is happening, Saanvi is drawn into the mood of the room. She stares at a dark red rectangle, weeping.

Koharu's flat experience of tasting wine involves sophisticated and accurate evaluations. But these evaluations emanate from her explicit judgments. And these judgments run via Koharu's sophisticated base of knowledge associating various properties of the taste profile of wine and various ways of evaluating and classifying a wine's quality. But the *experience* is neither good nor bad – it has neither phenomenal value nor phenomenal disvalue. This is because Koharu's experience lacks essentially affective evaluative phenomenal properties. By contrast, Saanvi's experience of Rothko in London involves very little in the way of cognitive evaluation. This is not to say that an education in Rothko would be of no use to Saanvi. Such an education might enhance her experience of the paintings. But in our case, Saanvi is not making any explicit judgments. She is simply experiencing a range of emotions caused by and directed at a painting. Nonetheless, Saanvi's experience is highly valuable. I submit this is so in part because Saanvi's experience contains a range of rich essentially affective evaluative properties.

I am not alone in suggesting such an interpretation.

Dan Moller (2011, 11) asks us to imagine judging that one has done something wrong, but failing – thanks to the passage of time, perhaps – to have any of the normal bodily and emotional sensations we associate with guilt. Moller writes, 'You may be continuously disposed to avow that you did wrong . . . Now ask, how awful is the guilt when the sensations are absent? And the answer, I take it, can only be 'Not at all'' (11).

Roger Crisp considers someone who appreciates the intricacies of Jane Austen's syntax but without enjoyment (where 'enjoyment' is Crisp's term for the high-level determinable property all positively valenced experiences share). Regarding such a case, Crisp avers that on reflection, the hedonist (which is what he is) 'should conclude that pleasureless appreciation is without value for the individual herself, though of course it may make for, say, a better human life, or add to the aesthetic value instantiated in the history of the universe in some way' (2006, 434).

The cases indicate the plausibility of [Affective-Evaluative Claim].[3] So we are making progress. But more complicated issues await.

Notes

1 Michael Chabon's description of nostalgia (from a *New Yorker* piece on nostalgia, see Chabon 2017) is better than I could do:

> Nostalgia, to me, is not the emotion that follows a longing for something you lost, or for something you never had to begin with, or that never really existed at all. It's not even, not really, the feeling that arises when you realize that you missed out on a chance to see something, to know someone, to be a part of some adventure or enterprise or milieu that will never come again. Nostalgia, most truly and most meaningfully, is the emotional experience – always momentary, always fragile – of having what you lost or never had, of seeing what you missed seeing, of meeting the people you missed knowing, of sipping coffee in the storied cafés that are now hot-yoga studios. It's the feeling that overcomes you when some minor vanished beauty of the world is momentarily restored, whether summoned by art or by the accidental enchantment of a painted advertisement for Sen-Sen, say, or Bromo-Seltzer, hidden for decades, then suddenly revealed on a brick wall when a neighboring building is torn down. In that moment, you are connected; you have placed a phone call directly into the past and heard an answering voice.

2 For a different way of thinking about how emotions might involve action-tendencies as well as possess a kind of evaluative content, see Scarantino (2014).

3 A quick word about my methodology here. Such cases are a fundamental part of my elucidation of an account of the value within consciousness. This is because my aim is to *demonstrate* the presence of non-derivative value. Here I follow Mill and others in thinking that, as Mill put it, 'Whatever can be proved to be good, must be so by being shewn to be a means to something admitted to be good without proof' (1863/2008, Chapter 1).

7 The importance of phenomenal character

> The objective world simply *is*, it does not *happen*. Only to the gaze of my consciousness, crawling upward along the life line of my body, does a section of this world come to life as a fleeting image in space which continuously changes in time.
>
> (Hermann Weyl)

Some of my friends who work in the philosophy of mind and cognitive science will roll their eyes at Weyl's lovely passage. There is a worry that all this talk of consciousness as somehow different from the objective world suggests a creeping dualism, a view of the subjective world as inexplicable by the lights of our one and only epistemic exemplar: science. But the metaphysics of consciousness is beside the present point. Weyl's passage, to my mind at least, evokes the wonder of the subjective viewpoint that consciousness constitutes. The idea I'm exploring is that there is non-derivative value present within consciousness. That idea is consistent with a denial of dualism, or any other position on the metaphysics of consciousness. Consider, for example, the following passage due to consciousness's most ruthless science-first explicator, Daniel Dennett. In the passage Dennett is considering what our perspective might be once science has explained the ways consciousness is of a piece with the other parts of a scientifically tractable view of the world.

> If conscious experience were 'reduced' somehow to mere matter in motion, what would happen to our appreciation of love and pain and dreams and joy? . . . let us remind ourselves of what has happened in the wake of earlier demystifications. We find no dimunition of wonder; on the contrary, we find deeper beauties and more dazzling visions of the complexity of the universe than the protectors of mystery ever

> conceived. . . . When we understand consciousness – when there is no more mystery – consciousness will be different, but there will still be beauty, and more room than ever for awe.
>
> (1991, 25)

The point is that in claiming consciousness has non-derivative value, one need not be thereby protecting the mystery of consciousness. Nor need one deny that consciousness may present an especially difficult case for scientific explanation. Whatever the case regarding the relationship between scientific progress and the explanatory mysteries surrounding consciousness, the claims I make about the value of consciousness deserve consideration – for my case for these claims does not depend on any purported resistance to scientific explanation.

Even so, one might understandably complain that my case thus far has neglected the rich contributions non-conscious processes make to mental life. Notice, for example, that the main claim defended so far – [Affective-Evaluative Claim] – is explicitly restricted to mental events or processes that possess phenomenal character. Might non-conscious events or processes also bear non-derivative value?

Presently I argue that the answer is no. The view I defend here is that it is *only* essentially affective evaluative phenomenal properties that are necessary and sufficient for (some) non-derivative value in a subject's mental life. We can call this the strong evaluative claim.

> [Strong Evaluative Claim] It is necessary and sufficient for the presence of some (non-derivative) value in a subject's mental life that the mental life contain episodes with essentially affective evaluative phenomenal properties.

Some readers may wonder: why care about this issue? Let us revert back to the kind of problem cases I discussed at this book's beginning. Here is a short story illustrating the kind of problem case that renders this issue salient.

> In the not-too-distant future, shadowy labs associated with very rich internet-savvy corporations begin to inform us they have done it – they have created artificially intelligent robots. These robots are roughly as intelligent as healthy adult human beings, and they prove useful for a wide range of tasks. For example, some of them prove highly useful as childminders. The busy rich are happy leaving their kids with their robot carers, who ultimately prove more resourceful and more empathetic than the parents themselves. And of course the kids love their

> robot carers, who come pre-programmed with far more energy than their parents to put up with the games, stories, and general hijinks that animate child life.
>
> Search the parental Q&A websites of the not-too-distant future, and you find dozens of threads on the same theme. It seems that the robot childminders sometimes make requests of the parents – they ask not to be turned off for the evening, or they ask if they can take the children on trips a bit further from home than the parents want. The children tend to side with the robots, of course. The parents are confused. They not only want to figure out how to manage these situations, but they also wonder if they are being cruel to the robots in denying their requests.
>
> Of course, as is familiar from family decisions about sick pets, the hardest times surround the decision to recycle or replace a robot that ages poorly – a robot with a broken part, or a robot with an outdated operating system. Some parents face severe guilt regarding such decisions. These tend to be the parents who are convinced that – in spite of the agnosticism that current science counsels – these robots have conscious mental lives. It seems there is a pattern of reasoning that is widely shared in our future society. If the robot is conscious, then it is a moral violation, and a grievous harm to the robot, to deny its requests for frivolous reasons, to recycle it for economic reasons, and so on.

I take it the pattern of reasoning present in this story will be familiar to many readers. Most of us have seen movies illustrating the issue. If the non-derivative value present in our mental lives does not depend upon phenomenal consciousness, then the parents of the future are misguided to worry about the issue. Of course, if we assume that these robots have minds of some kind, then it looks like these robots at least have non-conscious evaluative mental events. But if the non-derivative value present in our mental lives depends upon consciousness, then the question of robot consciousness becomes very important – roughly as important as we already think it is.

So I suggest that the pre-theoretical view is that consciousness is important for the kind of value at issue, and that an argument for this view would be both useful and important. What kind of argument might that be?

When we ascribe consciousness to an entity, we ascribe a certain kind of awareness to the entity. We affirm that there is *something* it is like for this entity to be aware of the things of which it is aware. Permit a metaphorical question: where might we locate this *something*? We locate it in the mental life of the subject. The conscious subject's mental life contains a feature – there is something it is like for her to be aware of things – that the non-conscious entity's mental life lacks.

The trick is to say a bit more about this feature. In my view, the notion we need is related to a notion sometimes called 'acquaintance.' It is not exactly this notion – for many view acquaintance as an essentially epistemic relation. A subject's acquaintance with objects and properties via conscious experience of them is thought to be critical for an explanation of how she comes by knowledge of these objects and properties. The notion we need is not necessarily epistemic. I will call it 'presence.' My idea is that of all the events that constitute a subject's mental life, those events presented to her within consciousness are special. Those events are present to her. As Bertrand Russell might have put it, they are *before her mind* in a certain way. Furthermore, there is an important relationship between presence and there being something it is like. In short, the property of what-it-is-like-ness that an item of conscious experience essentially possesses is constitutive of the presence of that item before an agent's mind.

A related claim is that items outside of conscious experience lack this presence: consciousness is necessary and sufficient for presence. Are there counterexamples to this claim? Enterprising philosophers may succeed where I have failed. But I cannot find any.

In virtue of a subject being phenomenally conscious, a subject's conscious experiences are present to her in a unique way. Another way of putting this is that a conscious experience presents things to the subject of the experience in a way no other mental or non-mental item does.

It turns out this is very important for a defense of [Strong Evaluative Claim]. The reason is that some mental item's being non-derivatively valuable requires not just essentially affective evaluative properties, but phenomenal versions of these properties – properties that secure presence to the subject.

To see why one might accept this last point, consider an example of Connie Rosati's: a world is created that is full of beauty, and one person capable of experiencing this beauty is placed there. But there is a catch: 'as befits the world around her, she is a beautiful person, only she is endlessly sleeping' (2008, 334). Rosati's question at this point is whether beauty (and assuming beauty is good, whether good) is occurring in her life. She considers two answers. According to the first, beauty (or good) occurs in one's life so long as it occurs 'in the time and place in which' one lives. Rosati notes this answer has unattractive consequences. Not only could we sleep or be comatose for the entirety of a life 'in which a good deal of good occurs,' it would seem we should treat the comatose differently than we do.

> We ought, other things equal, to redecorate meticulously the rooms of the permanently comatose, pipe beautiful music into their rooms, send

> in the clowns. To be sure, we will promote more good by expending our energies elsewhere. But the suggestion that we could have *any* reason to promote good occurring in the lives of the permanently comatose, at least in this sense, is dubious at best.
>
> (335)

The second answer Rosati considers has it that good occurs in a subject's life if the time and place conditions hold, and in addition the subject is conscious of the good. This answer is clearly better, but it might suffer from problems as well. For suppose, as Rosati does, that the Beauty awakens, becomes conscious of all the beauty and good in her world, 'yet takes no pleasure in the beauty around her; it is a matter of indifference to her' (337). What should we say about this kind of case?

At this point Rosati considers a more sophisticated answer, due to Donald Regan. It is worth quoting Regan here. For context, note that he is considering events like the conscious appreciation of a beautiful sunset.

> [W]hat is really valuable (non-relatively) is the appreciative engagement of the subject with a worthy object. The subject's pleasure is relevant because pleasure is an inevitable concomitant, and therefore a sign, of the right sort of engagement. But it is the engagement of the subject and appropriate object that is valuable. To my mind, when there is the right sort of engagement, we could as well say that the value created is value 'for' the sunset . . . as insist that the value is 'for' the subject. . . . But in fact, the real value is neither 'for' the subject nor 'for' the object. The value is just there, in a whole to which both subject and object make an indispensable contribution.
>
> (2004, 221)

Regan's view is explicitly patterned after G.E. Moore's, and depends on the Moorean view that goodness is simple and unanalyzable and inheres in organic wholes (such as the subject-object whole of considering subject and considered sunset). Rosati is not taken by the Moorean view, and goes on to develop an interesting view of a different kind of good, namely *good-for*, that she takes to be irreducible to good period occurring in one's life.

But let us put aside further discussion of Rosati's view on good-for. At present I wish to observe that there is a view here that neither Rosati nor Regan (nor Moore) adequately consider, which seems to me the right view concerning non-derivative value occurring in a subject's life. This is the view indicated by the [Strong Evaluative Claim]. In short, non-derivative value occurs in the life of a subject when the subject has experiences with affective, evaluative phenomenal character.

This view gets both the sleeping Beauty case and the indifferent Beauty case right. This view can remain agnostic regarding the Moorean view that there is value inherent in many of the items a subject experientially engages. It can remain agnostic as well on the Moorean view that experiential engagement with valuable items is much more valuable than evaluative experience alone.

With that said, however, it is worth considering this last Moorean claim. I explain why in the next chapter.

8 Contra Moore on an important point

> In such a case the poetry runs underground. The observer (poor soul, with his documents!) is all abroad. For to look at the man is but to court deception. We shall see the trunk from which he draws his nourishment; but he himself is above and abroad in the green dome of foliage, hummed through by winds and nested in by nightingales. And the true realism were that of the poets, to climb up after him like a squirrel, and catch some glimpse of the heaven for which he lives.
>
> And, the true realism, always and everywhere, is that of the poets: to find out where joy resides, and give it a voice far beyond singing.
>
> For to miss the joy is to miss all . . . the personal poetry, the enchanted atmosphere, that rainbow work of fancy that clothes what is naked and seems to ennoble what is base . . . no man lives in the external truth, among salts and acids, but in the warm, phantasmagoric chamber of his brain, with the painted windows and the storied walls.
>
> (Robert Louis Stevenson)

Although I am not claiming that evaluative experience is the only bearer of non-derivative value in the *world*, I do give it a central role in accounting for the value present in a subject's *mental life*. One might grant this while pressing the following worry. Following G.E. Moore, one might think that while evaluative experience has *some* value on its own, the amount is very little. If that is right, then one will think I am wasting everyone's time in building an account of the basis of value within consciousness. One might also worry that an upcoming task – to account for the ways the value within consciousness varies – is Quixotic. For if the amount of value at issue here is, in the end, very little, why think such reflection could help us think through the moral problem cases that motivate this book?

In the *Principia Ethica*, Moore was concerned to undermine hedonism – that is, 'the principle that nothing is good but pleasure' (sec. 36, para 1), or 'the doctrine that pleasure *alone* is good as an end' (sec. 37, para 1) – while upholding a central role for certain forms of consciousness in the constitution of non-derivative value (or good). One can see both concerns present in this important passage.

> By far the most valuable things, which we know or can imagine, are certain states of consciousness, which may be roughly described as the pleasures of human intercourse and the enjoyment of beautiful objects. No one, probably, who has asked himself the question, has ever doubted that personal affection and the appreciation of what is beautiful in Art or Nature, are good in themselves; nor, if we consider strictly what things are worth having *purely for their own sakes*, does it appear probable that any one will think that anything else has *nearly* so great a value as the things which are included under these two heads. I have myself urged in Chap. III. (§ 50) that the mere existence of what is beautiful does appear to have *some* intrinsic value; but I regard it as indubitable that Prof. Sidgwick was so far right, in the view there discussed, that such mere existence of what is beautiful has value, so small as to be negligible, in comparison with that which attaches to the *consciousness* of beauty. This simple truth may, indeed, be said to be universally recognised. What has *not* been recognised is that it is the ultimate and fundamental truth of Moral Philosophy. That it is only for the sake of these things – in order that as much of them as possible may at some time exist – that any one can be justified in performing any public or private duty; that they are the raison d'être of virtue; that it is they – these complex wholes *themselves*, and not any constituent or characteristic of them – that form the rational ultimate end of human action and the sole criterion of social progress: these appear to be truths which have been generally overlooked.
>
> (sec. 113, para 1)

Moore would deny that evaluative experience is sufficient for the presence of some non-derivative value in a subject's mental life, but he would agree that it is necessary. However, it is important for Moore that 'the ultimate and fundamental truth of Moral Philosophy' is about complex wholes comprised of experiences and their objects. Moore held that 'the intrinsic value of a whole is neither identical with nor proportional to the sum of the value of its parts' (sec. 111, para 2). Furthermore, he held that evaluative experiences on their own were of little value. For Moore, goodness was in the world, and consciousness was, in the main, merely the subject's form of access to, or appreciation of, that goodness.

One reason Moore seems to have thought this stems from his judgment about cases of inappropriate experiential evaluation. Consider the following passage.

> [B]y saying that different emotions are *appropriate* to different kinds of beauty, we mean that the whole which is formed by the consciousness of that kind of beauty *together with* the emotion appropriate to it, is better than if any other emotion had been felt in contemplating that particular beautiful object. Accordingly we have a large variety of different emotions, each of which is a necessary constituent in some state of consciousness which we judge to be good. All of these emotions are essential elements in great positive goods; they are *parts* of organic wholes, which have great intrinsic value. But it is important to observe that these wholes are organic, and that, hence, it does not follow that the emotion, *by itself*, would have any value whatsoever, nor yet that, if it were directed to a different object, the whole thus formed might not be positively bad. And, in fact, it seems to be the case that if we distinguish the emotional element, in any aesthetic appreciation, from the cognitive element, which accompanies it and is, in fact, commonly thought of as a part of the emotion; and if we consider what value this emotional element would have, *existing by itself*, we can hardly think that it has any great value, even if it has any at all. Whereas, if the same emotion be directed to a different object, if, for instance, it is felt towards an object that is positively ugly, the whole state of consciousness is certainly often positively bad in a high degree.
>
> (sec. 114, para 2)

Moore has evaluative experience as important in partially constituting a highly valuable organic whole. But the experience on its own may be of little or even no value. After asserting an intuition to this effect, in the earlier passage Moore further supports this view by claiming that a case of an inappropriately evaluative experience creates an organic whole that is highly bad.

I think Moore's intuition about an emotion on its own is wrong. And I think that Moore's case of an inappropriately evaluative experience does not support this view, but rather undermines it. In thinking these things, I need not deny all of Moore's claims about organic wholes. It may be true that organic wholes have value that is not a simple sum of their parts. The arguments I am about to offer concern only the value that essentially affective evaluative experiences have on their own. The arguments are intended to be responsive to Moore's picture. They are based in cases.

The joy of the wicked

Imagine a wicked man – a man with all of the traits and vices you find most loathsome, whether these be greed, callousness, arrogance, sloth, jealousy, absence of shame, poor personal hygiene, poor taste in fashion, an unsophisticated sense of humor, or whatever. Now imagine that this is a man well-suited to his time and place in the sense that no matter how wickedly this man acts, things work out for the best. His sloth is not punished. His greed leads to great wealth. His arrogance and absence of shame is celebrated in the press. His poor taste is reinforced by the sycophants who cluster around him. This man habitually harms other people, but instead of feeling remorse, he feels a sense of strength, freedom and power. When he reflects on his life, he experiences a deep sense of joy and contentment, and something akin to gratitude, though he feels this as directed to his own person and his own perceived strengths. What's more, in terms of mood, he is generally a happy, upbeat person – his days are full of positive experiential episodes such as finding mirth in the struggles of the poor, great intrigue and a sense of accomplishment at his job, and powerful but enjoyable lust directed towards women he serially abuses.

What is the upshot? We revile such a case, and with good reason. But the reason is not, I submit, that the wicked man's positive experiences are not, considered independently of context, non-derivatively valuable. Nor is the reason solely that the inappropriateness of much of this man's positive experience partially constitutes a very bad organic whole. I submit that one important reason for our revulsion is that this man's experience in its context constitutes a degradation of something highly non-derivatively valuable. These positive experiences are located very close to the things we hold most dear about our lives and our persons. There is very little as good as the purity of an experience of accomplishment or the finding of mirth in some event, provided we feel (as the wicked man does) that the accomplishment is genuine, the event truly funny. Our attitude to the wicked man's good experiences is not disanalogous to the revulsion some feel when a cherished religious artifact, or a great work of art, is desecrated. The artifact is not thereby rendered disvaluable, though within the broader context something of great disvalue has happened. And the explanation of this is, in part, due to the fact that the original artifact was highly non-derivatively valuable. So, too, with the wicked man's evaluative experiences.

The deceived sufferer

Imagine a healthy human adult, otherwise normal save one thing. This person – imagine they are on business in France, while their family

> remains in Finland – has just heard of the death of a child, and they believe it to be their child. Imagine, further, that there is no way for this person to discover their belief is false for a few days – perhaps not until they travel back to Finland. (Say that this tale is set in the days of yore.) This person's grief is, of course, every bit as extreme as if their child had actually died. And they will have to endure days of this grief, even though there is nothing in the world to support their grief.

What is the upshot? We feel a high degree of empathy for this person. Moreover, we should feel empathy for this person. What they are going through, during those days, is truly terrible. Those will probably be some of the worst days of that person's life. If so – if our empathy is well-founded, and if these days will, as seems plausible, be very bad days in that person's life – then this is largely because of the intensity and extremity of the evaluative experiences this person undergoes during those days.

> **The beautiful life**
>
> There are two versions of this case. One is based on the film *A Beautiful Life*, in which a father protects (or deceives) his son from the horrors of the concentration camp they are in by systematically making out that things are not horrible, but happy, beautiful, interesting, and so on. In this case focus on the son, who has a long series of positive, seemingly meaningful experiences in spite of the fact that the world around the boy does not warrant these experiences. The second version involves a ruthlessly – almost delusionally – optimistic person living in a squalorous, violent, poverty-stricken, crime-ridden, corrupt, racism-infused city. This person remains generally upbeat, and also undergoes a long series of positive, seemingly meaningful experiences that are deeply at odds with the world around her.

What is the upshot? The first version of this case is not the cleanest for my purposes, insofar as there are elements of one's child-rearing responsibilities and elements attached to the protection of one's children that muddy the moral. Even so, I think this case offers some support for the claim that positive evaluative experiences are highly valuable whether or not they correspond to the world in the right kind of way. The second case gives a clearer example. We might want the ruthless optimist to be a bit more savvy, to experience a bit more righteous anger in her circumstances, and so on. But it is hard to deny that in virtue of her optimism, this person has access to items of high non-derivative value. These items are her evaluative experiences. Indeed, I think most of us wish we were at least a little more optimistic than we are, in part because we know this would make available more valuable experiences – even if we think the world as it is does not warrant more optimism.

> **The part-time experience machine**
>
> Imagine an experience machine like the one Nozick (1974) introduced – a machine that you 'plug into,' 'that could give you any experience (or sequence of experiences) you might desire' (1989, 104). Nozick presented the machine, in part, to combat hedonism. For this reason the choice he offered involved the choice to plug into the machine *for the rest of your life*. I am not here combatting hedonism, though, and I don't need such an extreme choice. Imagine instead that you can plug into the machine for thirty-minute increments, as and when you have the time and energy. Add whatever features you like to the machine's operations – maybe you can enact whole alternative narratives that pause when you exit the machine and resume when you re-enter. Or maybe the machine simply gives you extremely positive experiences, whatever these might be, in thirty-minute bursts.

What is the upshot? I would gladly enter the machine, and I think most of my friends would as well. The reason is that there is clearly something very attractive about the idea of this machine, no matter how 'empty' the contents of one's experiences therein turn out to be. What is attractive, I submit, is that the experience machine gives one access to items of great non-derivative value. If we had such machines – instead of the garbage machines we currently use that give us access to little more than the misery of social media – our lives would be much improved. All else being equal, it's foolish to turn down such access.

The upshot of all of this is that Moore was wrong. Evaluative experiences can, on their own, constitute items of great value.

I think this is an important conclusion. But a word of caution is in order. In a wonderful paper, Mark Johnston considers an anecdote of Martin Buber's involving Buber's childhood self and a horse. In short, Buber's attention moved from the joy of grooming the horse to the joyful experience. Johnston characterizes the anecdote as a dramatization of 'a certain kind of ethical and epistemological fall from grace' (2001, 202), involving what he calls *the pornographic attitude*. Johnston explains:

> [T]he shift from looking at her, say with pleasure and interest, to absorption with one's pleasure and interest. In that moment she recedes, becomes a thing for the sake of one's pleasure and interest. As this

> goes on one attends to how she looks only in so far as it excites one's pleasure and interest. *She* has been reduced to a serviceable source of pleasure and interest. We are on the verge of an ethical and epistemological fall when this way of responding to others gets ossified into a stance or default attitude. Calling this fallen state 'the pornographic attitude' is intended to highlight the error of mentalizing affect. Instead of affect being a way in which the appeal and repulsiveness of other things and other people makes itself manifest, the affective states themselves become the focus of attention, as if affective engagement were an interior, private sensation detachable from one's being taken with or repelled by things.
>
> (2001, 203)

In arguing for the non-derivative value of certain kinds of conscious experience, I am aware of the danger of encouraging an overly pornographic attitude. I actually do not think the direction of attention to pleasant features of an experience is necessarily morally objectionable. Neither does Johnston, who immediately qualifies the passage by nothing there is nothing wrong, for example, with adjusting the shower's heat 'so that it pleases me' (203). The key is to find the right balance between an appreciation of the value inherent in one's experience and the non-experiential value one's experience makes present to one. That is more or less difficult to achieve depending on the case, e.g., in the case of bodily pleasures, there is often a nice consilience between pleasurable experience and the presentation of one's body as an item capable of bearing value. The point I wish to make here is simply that an emphasis on the non-derivative value present within consciousness need not be taken to encourage Johnston's pornographic attitude – at least not overmuch.

9 Hedonism about the value within consciousness

Socrates:	Would you consider that there was still anything wanting to you if you had perfect pleasure?
Protarchus:	Certainly not.
Socrates:	Reflect; would you not want wisdom and intelligence and forethought, and similar qualities? Would you not at any rate want sight?
Protarchus:	Why should I? Having pleasure I should have all things.
Socrates:	Living thus, you would always throughout your life enjoy the greatest pleasures?
Protarchus:	I should.
Socrates:	But if you had neither mind, nor memory, nor knowledge, nor true opinion, you would in the first place be utterly ignorant of whether you were pleased or not, because you would be entirely devoid of intelligence.
Protarchus:	Certainly.
Socrates:	And similarly, if you had no memory you would not recollect that you had ever been pleased, nor would the slightest recollection of the pleasure which you feel at any moment remain with you; and if you had no true opinion you would not think that you were pleased when you were; and if you had no power of calculation you would not be able to calculate on future pleasure, and your life would be the life, not of a man, but of an oyster or pulmo marinus. Could this be otherwise?
Protarchus:	No.
Socrates:	But is such a life eligible?
Protarchus:	I cannot answer you, Socrates; the argument has taken away from me the power of speech.

(from Plato's *Philebus* [trans. Benjamin Jowett])

Let's return to the case of Billy and Mrs. Ruffles. That was a mundane case of competing miseries. Billy had the thought that Mrs. Ruffles is just a dog, and I suggested that behind this thought was another: that because she was just a dog her misery was somehow not as bad, not as disvaluable, as Billy's. Most human beings who consider the issue will have this thought, and most will think it is actually true. Later in this book I will suggest that it is not at all clear that this thought is true. For now, however, I want to observe that this kind of thought raises an interesting question that an account of the value within consciousness ought to address. How are we to compare the value present within different experiences?

In order to think about questions of comparison, we need good models of the way value appears within consciousness. The most worked-out models we currently have come from various versions of hedonism. So I want to work my way into questions of comparison by looking at hedonistic models of the value within consciousness.

As I have done, hedonism gives pride of place to evaluative experience. There are various forms of hedonism, so there are various ways one might give evaluative experience pride of place. To take just two examples, hedonistic utilitarianism defines *right action* in terms of the generation of a balance of positive experience over negative experience. Hedonism about *well-being* understands the constitution of well-being as a matter of the positive and negative experiences that occur within a life (and there are different ways one may conceptualize the contributions positive and negative experiences make). I am not here concerned with hedonism about right action, or about well-being. I am concerned with hedonistic models of the value within consciousness, or as I will often call it, 'phenomenal value.'

The British utilitarian Jeremy Bentham offers a relatively simple model of phenomenal value. According to Bentham (1789), experiences of pleasure and pain are necessary and sufficient for whatever phenomenal value there is. Bentham characterizes amounts of phenomenal value in terms of 'dimensions of value.' Bentham discusses six dimensions, but four of these have to do not with the phenomenal value present in an experience, but with the ways an action might bring about pleasure or pain.[1] The two dimensions closely linked to amounts of phenomenal value are the intensity of a pleasurable or painful experience, and its duration. On Bentham's view, then, the value within consciousness at a time inheres in its positivity and negativity, which is graded according to the intensity of the pleasure. The value within consciousness over longer windows of time is merely additive, graded according to the duration of the valenced experiences one has at shorter windows of time. At least regarding discrete experiences, then, there are two fundamental dimensions to phenomenal value. And they fit together in a straightforward way.[2]

There is something attractive about this view. Certainly some sensory pleasures seem better than others, and many of the best ones are very intense. The same seems true regarding pains and disvalue. Intense pains are typically no fun. But although Bentham's model seems to get some instances of sensory pleasures and pains correct, the model is inadequate on more than one front.

First, in its appeal to intensity as a dimension of all positive experiences the model is phenomenologically inadequate. Intensity seems plausibly applied to many sensory experiences, but much evaluative experience is non-sensory. Consider, for example, some from Bentham's discussion. In discussing the kinds of pleasure that exist, he mentions the pleasures of power, and the pleasures of piety. The former 'are the pleasures that accompany the persuasion of a man's being in a condition to dispose people, by means of their hopes and fears, to give him the benefit of their services' (1789, chap 5, para 9). The latter are pleasures 'that accompany the belief of a man's being in the acquisition or in possession of the good-will or favour of the Supreme Being' (1789, chap 5, para 10). I do not disagree that positive experiences can be connected to possession or exercise of power, or to thoughts and imaginings about a supreme being and one's relationship to it. But these are complex kinds of experience, involving cognition, emotion, imagination, perception, and more in diverse interrelations. It does not seem like the positivity of the experiences in these classes is well-described in terms of degrees of intensity alone. For example, although some might count experiences of reflection on the supreme being's nature as among the best possible experiences, it is dubious that the intensity of such reflection is the reason. Or, to take a different example due to Roger Crisp, the experience of listening to a Debussy étude may be phenomenally better in some sense than the decidedly more intense experience of adrenalin one gets from the day's first cigarette (Crisp 2006, 632). Or, to press the point further than strictly necessary, consider a passage from William Boyd's novel *Any Human Heart*.

> The pleasures of my life here are simple – simple, inexpensive and democratic. A warm hill of Marmande tomatoes on a roadside vendor's stall. A cold beer on a pavement table of the Café de France – Marie Thérèse inside making me a sandwich au camembert. Munching the knob of a fresh baguette as I wander back from Sainte-Sabine. The farinaceous smell of the white dust raised by a breeze from the driveway. A cuckoo sounding the perfectly silent woods beyond the meadow. A huge grey, cerise, pink, orange and washed-out blue of a sunset seen from my rear terrace. The drilling of the cicadas at noon – the soft dialing-tone of the crickets at dusk slowly gathers. A good book, a hammock and a cold, beaded bottle of blanc sec. A rough red wine and steak frites. The cool, dark, shuttered silence of my bedroom – and,

> as I go to sleep, the prospect that all this will be available to me again, unchanged, tomorrow.
>
> (2009, 479)

Here Boyd's protagonist Logan Montstuart seems to have hit on one of life's nice patches. He has available a daily pattern of what seem to me to be excellent experiences. But intensity seems to have little to do with their excellence. So, to repeat: thinking of positive or negative experiences simply in terms of intensity fails to capture the ways many evaluative experiences are valuable. Many experiences are evaluative, and can be classified as in some sense positive or negative, even though intensity has little or even nothing to do with it.

Second, it is implausible that the duration of an experience contributes in the simple way Bentham envisages. Many good experiences come with certain time limits, in part because these experiences have a definitive shape. Some experiences – for example, witnessing the birth of one's child – could not be what they are unless they had time limits (see Sumner 1992). For such experiences, a model on which increased duration necessarily increases their value is plainly inadequate.

We find more complex models of phenomenal value in the work of Francis Hutcheson and John Stuart Mill. Both isolate a dimension in addition to duration and intensity, namely, an experience's quality (or what Hutcheson sometimes calls 'dignity'). As Mill puts it, 'some kinds of pleasure are more desirable and more valuable than others. It would be absurd that while, in estimating all other things, quantity is considered as well as quality, the estimation of pleasure should depend on quantity alone' (1863/2008, Chapter 2.4). And Hutcheson asserts:

> In comparing pleasures of different kinds, the value is as the duration and dignity of the kind jointly. We have an immediate sense of a dignity, a perfection, or beatifick quality in some kinds, which no intenseness of the lower kinds can equal, were they also as lasting as we could wish.
>
> (1755, I.ii.7.i, 117)

Mill organizes positive experiences into two classes: the higher and the lower pleasures. In giving grounds for this distinction, Mill makes reference to specific features of the actual structure of our mental life. He does so aware of the long-standing complaint against hedonism that in emphasizing the importance of pleasure – which some take to involve only the baser, sensory elements of experience – hedonism is 'a doctrine worthy only of swine' (1863/2008, Chapter 2). Mill expands upon the comparison between human and bovine mentality: 'Human beings have faculties more elevated than the animal appetites, and when once made conscious of them, do not regard anything as happiness which does not include their gratification' (Chapter 2). Elsewhere in the same chapter, he asserts the following.

> Next to selfishness, the principal cause which makes life unsatisfactory is want of mental cultivation. A cultivated mind – I do not mean that of a philosopher, but any mind to which the fountains of knowledge have been opened, and which has been taught in any tolerable degree, to exercise its faculties – finds sources of inexhaustible interest in all that surrounds it: in the object of nature, the achievements of art, the imaginations of poetry, the incidents of history, the ways of mankind, past and present, and their prospects on the future.
>
> (Chapter 2)

Mill argues, then, that experiences associated with the deployment of the 'higher faculties' are more desirable than experiences associated with lower faculties. That's an interesting proposition. But there are several ways in which this view of experiential quality is incomplete. What makes one faculty higher than another? Are the faculties sortable, as Mill thinks the pleasures are, into two distinct classes: higher and lower? Why are experiences associated with higher faculties deemed better or more valuable? Mill has little to say on these matters.[3]

Hutcheson's model has some similarities with Mill's, although it is more complex. He organizes positive experiences into four classes, graded by quality. The bottom class is similar to Mill's lower pleasures – here Hutcheson places the sensual, more bodily pleasures. The three classes above these might then be seen as a more detailed way of classifying the higher pleasures. At the second level Hutcheson places pleasures of, roughly speaking, the mind and intellect – pleasures of imagination, perception and contemplation of beauty, and of knowledge. Above these are pleasures associated with social interaction and seeing the happiness of close conspecifics. And at the highest level are moral pleasures, including those tied with one's sense of honor and virtue. In defense of this four-fold qualitative distinction, Hutcheson – like Mill – appeals to features of our nature. For Hutcheson, the kinds of mental capacities we actually possess are importantly related to the kinds and gradations of pleasures that, for us, exist. As he puts it in his (1769), 'the happiness of an insect or brute will only make an insect or brute happy. But a nature with further powers must have further enjoyments' (118).[4]

In providing a more complex model, Hutcheson might be taken to at least gesture towards a theory of what makes some faculties higher than others, or what makes them generate qualitatively better experiences. But few have found his model phenomenologically compelling. It is true that some experiences associated with virtuous action – with social interaction and the like – can be highly meaningful. But this is far from necessarily true. Nor is it clear that pleasures of the intellect are always qualitatively better than sensual pleasures, as critics of Mill have often noted (Riley 2008, 2009; Schmidt-Petri 2006).

I have observed problems with the models offered by Bentham, Hutcheson, and Mill. These problems are largely phenomenological: that is, I have not discussed the way these models understand how consciousness bears value. Before discussing that, then, it would be good to consider a hedonistic model that is not as clearly phenomenologically underwhelming.

A more recent hedonist account fits the bill. Interestingly this account, due to Roger Crisp (2006), is in a way simpler than the models considered thus far. Crisp maintains that there is only one dimension within phenomenal character that really matters, and that it is not intensity or duration or quality. Rather, what makes an experience good for the subject who has it is its being *enjoyable*. As Crisp says, 'this is the only "good-for-making" property there is' (623).

What, then, is it for an experience to be enjoyable? Crisp develops the idea that evaluative experience has a determinable-determinate structure. There are many different determinate ways to have enjoyable experiences; in spite of underlying differences, these experiences share the high-level determinable property of enjoyableness. Furthermore, Crisp maintains that this property comes in degrees:

> I can ask you to rank those experiences in terms of how enjoyable they are. Note that this is not asking you which you prefer, since you may have preferences which are not based on enjoyment. Nor is it asking which is better. It is asking you to rank the experiences according to the degree to which you enjoyed each.
>
> (629)

Crisp allows that enjoyableness is influenced by more determinate phenomenal properties. One experience may be (correctly) judged enjoyable to degree D in part because of more determinate properties such as intensity. But a different experience may be (correctly) judged enjoyable to degree D + 1 even though it lacks intensity, or has less intensity than the former experience. The relationship between the more determinate properties that constitute enjoyable experiences, and enjoyableness itself, is apparently complex. Consider, for example, Crisp's case of the novel and the lemonade:

> [I]magine someone who has just drunk a cool glass of lemonade and has also completed her first reading of Jane Austen's *Pride and Prejudice*. If we ask her to rank, on a scale of enjoyableness, the experience of drinking the lemonade against that of reading the novel, she may well rank the novel higher than the lemonade. Why? There is much more to this judgment than mere duration. There is nothing to prevent our judge's claiming that it would not matter how long the experience of enjoyable drinking could be prolonged: She would never enjoy it as much as she enjoyed the novel. For what she enjoyed in the novel was its wit, its beautiful syntax, and its exquisite delineation of character. The loss of such enjoyments (that is, enjoyable experiences) – in the context of her own life – could never be compensated for, in terms of enjoyment alone, by any amount of lemonade pleasure.
>
> (633)

In commenting that the reader's enjoyment comes in the context of the reader's own life, Crisp is allowing that the views – the knowledge base, values, etc. – of the subject can impact how enjoyable a certain kind of experience is for her. Crisp is here on to what is in my view a very deep insight regarding the structure of evaluative experience. As Crisp says, 'we refer to many more qualities than that of duration in explaining what we find enjoyable in our experiences' (633). Indeed, we refer to qualities that are sometimes context-dependent, sometimes idiosyncratic, sometimes dependent upon particular personal beliefs or values, and sometimes colored by what has come before and what is expected to come after – colored by the context of our own life.

Phenomenologically, then, Crisp's view is a clear improvement on earlier models. As Crisp would likely concede, the model is undeveloped in certain ways, most obviously regarding the relationship between the determinate properties constitutive of particular experiences and the high-level determinable of enjoyableness. This is in part because Crisp's main aim is to defend hedonism about well-being, rather than to perfectly chart the structure of evaluative experience. And it is in part an intentional choice by Crisp: given that the relationship between determinate properties and enjoyableness can vary by individual, Crisp regards the project of constructing 'some kind of objective scale for measuring the enjoyableness and hence the value of certain experiences, independently of the views of the subject' as 'merely a dream' (633).

I agree with this point as far as it goes. But I think it is nonetheless worth our while to think a bit more about this relationship between determinate and determinable within the structure of evaluative experience, and what it might imply for a model of phenomenal value. In this connection, notice the reasoning embedded in a portion of the Crisp quote cited earlier. Crisp talks of constructing a scale for measuring enjoyableness *and hence the value* of experiences. Something like this thought is present as an assumption in all of the hedonistic models considered in this chapter. It might help to raise it to the surface.

> [Hedonism About Phenomenal Value] In a particular way, phenomenal value inherits its structure from the valence of phenomenal character. The more positive an experience's phenomenal character, the more value the experience bears. The more negative an experience's phenomenal character, the less value (or the more disvalue) the experience bears.

That's an interesting set of propositions. I think a number of cases could be described that this general view captures well. But I am not sure [Hedonism About Phenomenal Value] captures the entire relationship between phenomenal character and phenomenal value. I have questions about the phenomenology implicit in it. And I have questions about the conception it offers regarding the way experiences bear value.

Regarding the phenomenology, it is worth asking whether valuable experiences can be cleanly and exhaustively described in terms of a placement upon a spectrum that measures degrees of positivity and negativity. As we have already seen, Crisp admits that there are many ways for combinations of determinate phenomenal properties to constitute enjoyable experiences. But, given how little Crisp thinks we can say about the relationship between determinable and determinate hedonic properties, it seems fair to ask whether the best phenomenology should posit one determinable, enjoyableness, that covers all the ways experiences have positive phenomenal character. Maybe a better phenomenology posits a plurality of ways, such that one determinable property cannot capture them all. (If this latter possibility is right, it may be somewhat misleading to speak in terms of phenomenal positivity and negativity. Perhaps the situation is more complex than such unidimensional language implies.)

Regarding the relationship between phenomenal character and phenomenal value, it is worth asking whether a change in an experience's valence is the only factor relevant to explaining changes in the value an experience bears. This worry can be highlighted by paying attention to the phenomenology of many of the emotions. Consider, for example, this passage from Robert Solomon's article 'Against Valence.'

> [P]leasure and pain do not form a polarity and are in no singular sense 'opposites.' Nor does the rich texture of most emotions allow us to

> assign a single 'valence' on the basis of pleasures and pains, even 'all things considered.' Anger can be very pleasurable, especially if it is righteous. Anger can be very painful, if it concerns an offense from a loved one. Anger can be very fulfilling on the one hand and nevertheless very painful at the same time, such as when one is winning a heated argument with a spouse or friend. Love is among the most pleasant of emotions, but it can also be the most painful. It is an essential datum in the study of emotions, this phenomenon of 'mixed feelings,' but this does not just mean one emotion coupled with another. Within an emotion there can be a number of different 'valences,' even in terms of the no longer simple dichotomy of pleasure and pain.
>
> (2003, 170)

One hedonist-friendly way of accommodating mixed feelings is to claim that they necessarily contain value and disvalue in virtue of the mix. But is this right? Is the value of some mixed feelings simply a function of so-called positively valenced elements within the experience? If you have your doubts, as I have mine, then you should be sympathetic to the thought that [Hedonism About Phenomenal Value] cannot be a full account of phenomenal value, even if it gets a number of cases right.

This is not, I hasten to add, anything yet like an argument against [Hedonism About Phenomenal Value]. I am only attempting to motivate the considerations that follow – considerations that I think push us beyond this venerable way of thinking about phenomenal value, towards something new. In the chapters that follow, I construct a model that fills in some of the gaps I think [Hedonism About Phenomenal Value] leaves, and that corrects some of the implicit phenomenology therein.

Notes

1 These were one's certainty that an action would bring about a pleasure or pain, the remoteness of pleasure or pain to an action, the fecundity of an action in bringing about pleasure or pain, and purity, or the ways that a pleasure might tend to be followed by a pain.

2 There is a lack of clarity here regarding how we might add the value of discrete experiences. Presumably, Bentham would want to say that the more good experiences, the better. But given that over finite windows of time, experiences with more duration will mean fewer experiences, it would seem that the Benthamite faces a trade-off between better, longer experiences and worse, more numerous experiences.

3 He does posit a sense of dignity as important in this connection, and avers that this sense of dignity is possessed

> in some, though by no means in exact, proportion to [one's] higher faculties, and which is so essential a part of the happiness of those in whom it is strong,

> that nothing which conflicts with it could be, otherwise than momentarily, an object of desire to them.
>
> (Chapter 2)

4 Dale Dorsey (2010) argues that Hutcheson was not actually a qualitative hedonist. According to Dorsey, these distinctions can ultimately be understood in terms of propensities to cause pleasures of greater intensity and duration: 'the quality of pleasure is only important insofar as the cooperation of our moral and evaluative senses increases the overall quantity of pleasure' (466). I am not convinced, but getting Hutcheson's actual view right is not my primary aim here (though see Strasser 1987). I aim to assess the prospects for a qualitative hedonist account of phenomenal value.

10 The bearers of phenomenal value

> But for me it was enough if, in my own bed, my sleep was so heavy as completely to relax my consciousness; for then I lost all sense of the place in which I had gone to sleep, and when I awoke at midnight, not knowing where I was, I could not be sure at first who I was; I had only the most rudimentary sense of existence, such as may lurk and flicker in the depths of an animal's consciousness; I was more destitute of human qualities than the cave-dweller; but then the memory, not yet of the place in which I was, but of various other places where I had lived, and might now very possibly be, would come like a rope let down from heaven to draw me up out of the abyss of not-being, from which I could never have escaped by myself: in a flash I would traverse and surmount centuries of civilization, and out of a half-visualized succession of oil-lamps, followed by shirts with turned-down collars, would put together by degrees the component parts of my ego.
>
> (Marcel Proust [trans. C.K. Scott Moncreiff])

Thus far I have used phrases like 'the value within consciousness,' or 'the value present in an experience.' These phrases are elliptical for the fact that something within conscious experience bears non-derivative value. My assumption, apparent in at least some of my language up to this point, has been that it is *experiences* that bear value. Is that right?

Philosophers have offered different proposals regarding the *bearers of value* (see, e.g., the discussion in Zimmerman 2015). But the differences are not very important for present purposes. To illustrate why, consider an experience that seems to bear value – the experience of hearing a friend's joke, finding it funny, and then laughing at it. One proposal is that properties are the fundamental bearers of value (Butchvarov 1989). On that proposal, what bears value might be said to be the property of undergoing that experience. A second proposal is that states of affairs are the fundamental bearers of value (Chisholm 1975). On that proposal, what bears value might be said to be the state of affairs of having that experience. A third proposal is that facts are the fundamental bearers of value (Ross 1930). On that proposal, what bears value might be said to be the fact that the subject had that experience. I'm thus not sure that it matters, but I'm attracted to a fourth proposal, namely that we should be pluralists about the bearers of value (see Rønnow-Rasmussen 2011, Chapter 10, for a defense). On this proposal, it is fine to speak of experiences themselves bearing value.

But what is an experience? A generic view is that an experience is the instantiation of at least one phenomenal property by a subject at a time. So, for example, I take a sip of water, and I feel a cool sensation on my tongue. The instantiation of that cool sensation by me at that time was an experience. That's easy enough. But things get more complicated when we try to apply the generic view to instantiations of more than one phenomenal property by a subject at a time, or over certain windows of time (since, after all, experiences at least seem to occupy or take up amounts of time). Right now I feel an ache in my thigh, I hear a car passing on a nearby street, I have a memory of crows sitting atop the old chapel opposite my office. Am I having three experiences or one conjoint experience? Suppose, having the memory of crows, I look up to the chapel roof as I type. The memory and then the act of looking seem to be related in some way. Are they parts of the same experience: perhaps temporal parts? Do experiences have parts? And if they do, how do they compose and decompose?

Call experiences that involve instantiations of a single phenomenal property 'simple experiences,' and experiences that involve instantiations of more than one phenomenal property 'complex experiences.' Obviously complexity comes in degrees – just think about the range of experiences of differing complexity towards which Proust's passage gestures – but I won't worry about that right now. What we need to know is what kind of structure complex experiences take, such that they qualify as actual experiences.

As a way into these issues, let me make two very plain observations. First, a subject's conscious experience at a time (and over time) typically involves a wide range of phenomenal properties. Second, some of these properties seem to be more closely connected to others, while some of these properties seem largely distinct from others. As Bennett and Hill put this second observation, 'An element of informed common sense is that some experiences of a subject at a time occur independently of other experiences undergone by that subject at that time' (2014, 233). Why are some experiences (or some phenomenal properties) more closely related – we might say more unified in some way – than others?

In an influential book on the unity of consciousness, Tim Bayne picks out a number of relations fit for doing work in connection with this question. One relevant kind of relation is that of representational unity, where 'conscious states are representationally unified to the degree that their contents are integrated with each other' (2010, 10). As Bayne notes, insofar as there are different ways to integrate contents (and different ways to think about integration), there may be many forms of representational unity. David Bennett and Christopher Hill (2014), for example, discuss a range of ways conscious contents are integrated. Sensory experience often integrates contents drawn from multiple modalities and attributes these contents to objects or events – they call this 'object binding unity.' A further kind of unity stems from the ways the mind represents objects and events as 'present in a shared spatial setting' (238). This is 'phenomenal spatial unity.' A unique kind of content integration might depend on the subject's accessing multiple contents or states within a single cognitive or introspective state (such as a judgment).

Bayne calls another kind of unity relation 'phenomenal unity.' To explicate this notion, Bayne distinguishes between specific conscious states and total conscious states (at a time). Specific conscious states can be explicated in terms of their phenomenal character, and their relation to total conscious states is one of subsumption. Total conscious states subsume specific conscious states, and 'a total conscious state is a state that is subsumed by nothing but itself, where one conscious state subsumes another if the former includes the latter as a "part" or "component"' (2010, 15). This relation of subsumption is a phenomenal relation – there is something it is like to undergo multiple specific conscious states conjointly.

> Consider . . . what it's like to hear a rumba playing on the stereo whilst seeing a bartender mix a mojito. These two experiences might be subject unified insofar as they are both yours. They might also be representationally unified, for one might hear the rumba coming from behind the bartender. But over and above these unities is a deeper and more primitive unity: the fact that these two experiences possess a *conjoint experiential character*. There is something it is like to hear the rumba, there is something it is like to see the bartender work, and there is something it is like to hear the rumba *while* seeing the bartender work. (10–11)

Although in my view the existence of phenomenal unity is introspectively apparent, Bayne's claim that this kind of unity is 'deeper and more primitive' has proven controversial. Consider, by contrast, Christopher Hill's Unity Pluralism Account. Hill advocates three theses. First, the multiple relations thesis, on which 'there is a large and diverse set of relations that can be said to unify conscious experiences' (2014, 501). Second, the partial unity thesis, on which 'the experiences that a single subject enjoys at a single time will in general have a large degree of unity, owing to the fact that pairs of experiences are linked by various unity relations' (502). Third, the disunity thesis, on which 'the experiences of subjects tend not to be totally unified' (502). Hill notes that in some cases a subject's specific experiences will be unified into something like Bayne's total conscious state, but this will not be in virtue of any relation of phenomenal unity. On Hill's view, it is not the case

> that experiences are always united by a single unity relation and that experiences are always linked by the members of set of relations . . . the experiences of a subject at a time will generally consist of 'islands' of experiences that are unified with each other but not with the constituents of other islands.
>
> (502)

The disagreement between Bayne and Hill generates an interesting and important debate regarding the unity of consciousness. But for our purposes, their agreement is more important – for they agree that there are multiple ways for parts of one's conscious field (both at a time and over time) to be legitimately unified.

Now recall our guiding question. What is an experience? I am following Bayne, Hill, and others in thinking that there are many legitimate ways for parts of one's conscious field to be unified, both at a time and over time. (I am leaving it open how many legitimate unity relations there are, and what their specific character will be.) To this, I add the plausible thought that when we speak of an experience as an item, we denote little more than the fact that parts of our conscious field seem unified in some way, either at a time or over time. Together these thoughts yield a pluralism about the composition of at least certain experiences – namely, the ones that require composition (i.e., the complex ones – the ones with proper parts). This kind of pluralism has struck many philosophers as attractive. Reflecting on our guiding question, for example, Tim Bayne has this to say:

> I am not convinced that there is any single way in which experiences should be individuated. Counting experiences is arguably more like counting the number of objects in a room or the number of events that took place during a meeting than it is like counting the number of beans in a dish: one has some idea of how to go about one's business, but the idea that there is only one way in which to proceed is somewhat farcical. The notion of a token experience is elastic, and different approaches to the individuation of experiences might be appropriate in different contexts.
>
> (2010, 24)

This seems right to me, although it remains to state my pluralist position with a little bit more precision. The central idea is as follows.

> **Pluralism**
>
> A subject S undergoes a complex experience E if S instantiates more than one phenomenal property (at a time or over time) and these properties are unified to some sufficient degree by at least one legitimate unity relation.

As I understand it, *pluralism* leaves open a number of issues that a full mereology of experience would need to address. It only states a minimal sufficient condition for the existence of a complex experience. It does not commit to any priority relationship between complex and non-complex experiences. It does not commit to any priority relationship between kinds of complex experiences, e.g., between total conscious experiences at a time and parts of total conscious experiences at a time. It is neutral regarding the possibility that some unity relations are prior, or more fundamental, or whatever, than others. It does not attempt to work out the compositional relationships between different unity relations, so it is silent on whether a complex experience E could be composed by phenomenal properties A and B bound by relation U1, properties B and C bound by U2, and so on.

Pluralism about complex experiences gives us some idea of the kinds of mental items that bear value. These are instantiations of phenomenal properties by subjects at certain times and over certain windows of time, so long as the properties constitutive of the experience are bound by legitimate unity relations.

Now, recall [Affective-Evaluative Claim], according to which the only experiences that bear value contain essentially affective evaluative phenomenal properties. These experiences will often contain more than just these properties, of course. What role do the other properties play in the way that an experience bears value? I take up this question in the next four chapters.

11 Thick experiences

> These people who have lost someone look naked because they think themselves invisible. I myself felt invisible for a period of time, incorporeal. I seemed to have crossed one of those legendary rivers that divide the living from the dead, entered a place in which I could be seen only by those who were themselves recently bereaved. I understood for the first time the power in the image of the rivers, the Styx, the Lethe, the cloaked ferryman with his pole. I understood for the first time the meaning in the practice of suttee. Widows did not throw themselves on the burning raft out of grief. The burning raft was instead an accurate representation of the place to which their grief (not their families, not the community, not custom, their grief) had taken them. On the night John died we were thirty-one days short of our fortieth anniversary. . . .
>
> We have no way of knowing that the funeral itself will be anodyne, a kind of narcotic regression in which we are wrapped in the care of others and the gravity and meaning of the occasion. Nor can we know ahead of the fact (and here lies the heart of the difference between grief as we imagine it and grief as it is) the unending absence that follows, the void, the very opposite of meaning, the relentless succession of moments during which we will confront the experience of meaninglessness itself.
>
> (Joan Didion)

Consider the experiences that, out of a set of all the experiences one has had, one would judge contain the most value. These experiences – for me, they might include a particularly great day of skiing, witnessing the birth of my children, the feeling of falling in love for the first time, the experience of moving with friends from a city I did not like to a city I loved – seem to vary quite a bit in terms of their more determinate properties. Even so, the reason that these experiences seem so valuable seems to have more to do with their determinate properties than with any degree of felt or experienced enjoyableness. What is important about these experiences is the particular sense of freedom one had on the mountain that day, the sun on nearby peaks, the difficulty associated with the labor and how you and your partner worked through it, her face when she saw the baby, what you felt when the midwife said 'here he is,' and so on. When I stress the importance of the more determinate properties, I mean to highlight the fact that what makes these experiences so good (and other experiences so bad) is their more determinate *shape*, and arguably their place within one's life.

This suggests that regarding phenomenal value, there is an important relationship between the more determinate properties of one's experiences and value – a relationship one might miss by focusing on a high-level determinable property (e.g., enjoyableness) these experiences might (or might not) share.

At this point I want to introduce a notion. I do so by analogy. Some philosophers talk of 'thick concepts' (see Kirchin 2013). These are concepts that essentially combine evaluation with non-evaluative descriptive content. So a thick concept does not characterize an item as simply good or bad, or an action as simply right, wrong, permissible, supererogatory, or whatever. A thick concept characterizes items and actions as banal, gracious, courageous, kind, fair, rude, gauche, etc. The key thing is simply that the concept combines and integrates the evaluative and the descriptive.

Now consider the notion of a 'thick experience': a set of (essentially affective) evaluative and non-evaluative phenomenal properties unified to some sufficient degree by at least one legitimate unity relation. Of course, most of our experiences are thick experiences. The smell of one's first cup of coffee is both pleasant and rich with the determinate properties of the coffee beans in use, and is often accompanied by a distinct mild thrill, a kind of anticipatory burst of the heightened awareness caffeine brings. The olfactory properties of the experience are as critical to the experience being what it is as are the evaluative properties.[1]

Here is a further claim. The value that a thick experience bears depends upon the experience being what it is. So the value that thick experiences bear depends in part upon their determinate properties – whether these are descriptive or evaluative. When I say *depends upon*, I have in mind a kind of explanatory relation philosophers call the 'grounding relation.' One way to express this relation is by use of the term 'in virtue of.' A thick experience E bears value in virtue of the properties that make E what it is.

Consider this claim in light of [Hedonism About Phenomenal Value]. That view involved claims that the more *positive* an experience's phenomenal character, the more value the experience bears, and vice versa for negativity and disvalue. Those claims seem straightforwardly true for thin evaluative experiences – experiences that involve only essentially affective evaluative properties. But it is not obvious that these claims extend cleanly to thick experiences. The reason is that the notions of positive and negative in play are meant to indicate (probably highly determinable) phenomenal properties. But if the value a thick experience bears is influenced by more than its valenced phenomenal properties, then [Hedonism About Phenomenal Value] is incomplete. (It's not thereby *false* – notice I avoided characterizing the view as a claim that the only way to influence phenomenal value was via valenced phenomenal character.)

The hedonist might wish to deny my previous claim that the value that a thick experience bears depends on the properties that make the experience what it is. Consider two natural ways of filling out a hedonist model of phenomenal value (here I'm following the same line of thought taken by Rønnow-Rasmussen 2011, 163–164). First, experiences bear value, but only in virtue of their hedonic properties. Second, it is not experiences that bear value, but only properties of experience, and in particular only hedonic properties. On either proposal, the non-hedonic is at best instrumentally relevant to phenomenal value, and the argument I'm making about the importance of the determinate shape of thick experiences can be resisted.

However, I think that either way of filling out a hedonistic model of phenomenal value has bad consequences. For one thing, these models treat parts of our evaluative experiences as irrelevant to the value these experiences bear. But these are often just the parts that seem necessary for the value borne. An experience that includes the evaluative properties associated with the smell of my first cup of coffee, but not the determinate olfactory and physiological properties of the experience, is an odd thing to contemplate. It might bear value – I have no problem with the conceivability of thin experiences made up only of evaluative properties – but it seems to do so in a very different way from my experience of smelling the coffee.

One might not like the coffee example. Episodes of grief are perhaps more compelling. Such episodes collect a wide range of complicated, difficult, terrible experiences – as the passages from Didion at this chapter's beginning indicate. The affective elements of these experiences are in some sense bad. But considered in abstract from the descriptive elements of the experience – one's awareness of who has been lost, one's awareness of the nature of the loss in the context of one's own life – such affective elements make little sense. If one were to undergo only the affective elements, perhaps because one suffers from some little-studied neurological disorder, one's experiences would be disvaluable. But they would be far less disvaluable than are experiences of grieving a lost loved one. It seems, then, that the more descriptive elements of evaluative experiences can influence, and are in many cases critical for, the way an experience bears value.

I think the more examples one considers, the more obvious it seems that the more determinate shape of an experience is critical for the value it bears. I elaborate upon this point in the next chapter.

Note

1 Regarding thick concepts, philosophers have gone several rounds arguing over whether the content can be disentangled into non-evaluative and (thin) evaluative components, or whether the content is fused or integrated in some way that renders the content irreducible to distinct components. That's an interesting debate, and we could imagine a parallel one regarding experiences. After all, the notion of binding is central to theories of many different psychological capacities, and one might wonder whether the evaluative is bound to the non-evaluative in such a way as to render thick experiences irreducible into components. But I'm not going to engage in that kind of debate. It doesn't matter for my purposes – for my notion of a thick experience does not appeal to essentially integrated contents, but rather to phenomenal properties that may be legitimately distinct so long as they are bound by a legitimate unity relation.

12 Meta-evaluative properties

> Of the many sensations of which my body had been the theater during three hours, not the least strange was the feeling I experienced on coming back into a normal condition. The recovery did not proceed gradually, but the whole outer and inner world of reality came back, as it were, with a bound. And for a moment it seemed strange. It was the sensation – only much intensified – which everyone has known on coming out into the light of day from an afternoon performance at a theater, where one has sat in an artificial light of gas and lamps, the spectator of a fictitious world of action. As one pours out with the crowd into the street, the ordinary world, by force of contrast with the sensational scenes just witnessed, breaks in upon one with almost a sense of unreality. The house, the aspects of the street, even the light of day appear a little foreign for a few moments. During these moments everything strikes the mind as odd and unfamiliar, or at least with a greater degree of objectivity. Such was my feeling with regard to my old and habitual self. During the period of intoxication the connection between the normal condition of my body and my intelligence had broken – my body had become in a manner a stranger to my reason – so that now on reasserting itself it seemed, with reference to my reason, which had remained perfectly sane and alert, for a moment sufficiently unfamiliar for me to become conscious of its individual and peculiar character. It was as if I had unexpectedly attained an objective knowledge of my own personality. I saw, as it were, my normal state of being with the eyes of a person who sees the street on coming out of the theater in broad day.
>
> (Havelock Ellis, quoting a friend's report of a mescaline experience)

Fair warning to readers: in this chapter I am largely concerned with phenomenology, the description of what certain experiences are like. The reason is that we have to get the right model of phenomenal value, and at least half of that is getting the right model of the kinds of experiences that have value. The other half, of course, is understanding how these experiences bear value. But the two are related. In this chapter I want to use some phenomenological considerations to press the point I made in the last chapter regarding the way that experiences bear value.

In the last chapter I introduced the notion of thick experiences. In this chapter I want to further qualify thick experiences by introducing the notion of meta-evaluative phenomenal properties. These are properties that help determine the phenomenal character of an experience. But they are not directed at features of the world. Rather, they are directed at features of one's experience, e.g., relationships between different aspects of a complex experience. It might be difficult to clearly transmit what I have in mind here. So allow me some room for illustration.

Consider the experience of trying a new substance. Visiting Taiwan, you learn of the betel nut – a stimulant that many people in Taiwan chew, whose effect has been described to me by my trusty office mate Hannah as similar to smoking ten cigarettes very quickly, but not quite. That doesn't sound great, but it sounds *interesting* – I'd like to try it (once). Many of us can recall experiences of trying a new substance, feeling a bit of a thrill as we do so. There is a particular kind of feeling, but that's not necessarily why we value the experience. The reason is that the feeling is indeed difficult to place. If we're lucky, the feeling is genuinely novel. That is, while you are having the experience there is an attempt to place – memory and imagination are engaged – and the fact that one fails is experienced as interesting, and perhaps as a kind of excursion into a region of experiential space that is uncharted. I want to say that there is a kind of value here, and it has little or nothing to do with the experience being pleasant. Maybe the feeling is unpleasant – you might value it for the same reason. The reason is *novelty*.

Consider the experience of finishing a novel – any decent novel will do. Finishing that novel, the attentive reader will be undergoing a range of experiences, most of them within the imaginative space one sets up surrounding the world of the novel. One will be balancing what is happening in the novel with expectations about what might happen that one has developed throughout the reading. One will be experiencing the emotions of various characters vicariously, depending perhaps on how intimately one identifies with them. One will be making judgments, and feeling attendant evaluative experiences, regarding complex trails of causation, thematic harmonies and disharmonies, instances of justice or injustice, as the plot pulls various threads together (or fails to). If one is lucky, one may be having an overarching epiphany, a deep sense of insight into either the author's intentions, the state of one's own world or life or character, or perhaps into all of these things almost at once. Reading a great novel is a beautiful, moving experience. And it is clear that many of the complex experiences one undergoes as one reads will possess relations of representational unity, such that one is able to undergo an experience dazzling in its complexity, and striking in the kind of thematic harmony tying many of the diverse threads within the experience together. I do not know the best way to put names on the kinds of meta-properties at issue. My best guess is that such an experience is valuable in part because meta-evaluative properties of *richness in complexity*, as well as *harmony in diversity*, are a part of what it is like to finish a great novel.

I am not the first person to notice that what I have called 'meta-evaluative properties' can be an important part of the phenomenal character of some experiences. In this connection, consider the experience of *enjoying pain*. This sometimes occurs in sexually charged contexts. Other times it occurs in the context of athletic challenge or achievement. Consider, too, under this general heading, enjoying the experience of various negative emotions, as happens when one watches a sad or frightening film. What is going on in such experiences?

I don't wish to take a determinate stand, but two interesting accounts are worth mentioning. Regarding the experience of enjoying negative emotions that art sometimes evokes, at least one philosopher has proposed that a certain meta-stance one takes towards one's experiences can help explain it. According to Susan Feagin (1983), the experience of negative emotions in the context of the contemplation of art is compensated for by experiences attached to this meta-stance. In an interesting review of work on the so-called paradox of tragedy, Aaron Smuts summarizes her view well.

> [T]he reason people want to experience tragedy is because they take pleasure in the experience, or more exactly, they take pleasure in the reactions they have to such fictions. The pleasure is in the meta-response, the response we have to our direct responses to the fiction. The particular meta-response that she thinks we find pleasurable is something of a self-congratulatory feeling – we are glad that we are the kind of person that can feel pity at the suffering of others.
>
> (2009, 49)

Feagin thus gives one example of a way that a complex experience involving some negative affect can be valuable in a surprising way.

Now consider so-called masochistic pleasures. Colin Klein (2014) offers a very interesting explanation of the goodness of these experiences. To get such pleasures more clearly in mind, Klein offers a useful list: wiggling a loose tooth, eating hot chilies, running a marathon, getting a tattoo, classical masochism (e.g., being whipped), slap and tickle masochism (e.g., hair-pulling or biting during sex), non-sexual masochism, obsessively dwelling on one's anger or jealousy, and the already considered experiences associated with the paradox of tragedy. Of the items on this list, Klein comments:

> In each case, we find people engaged in an activity that they sincerely claim is painful, and yet they also claim to find it pleasant. Further, there is good reason to think both avowals are true. The activity itself is unquestionably painful for people who *don't* find it pleasant. That's easy enough to confirm. Yet people don't *just* claim to find that painful feeling pleasant – they also pursue it. That is usually good evidence that someone is being sincere about finding something pleasant. So we have good evidence that the masochistic pleasures are real.
>
> (42–43)

There are of course various proposals regarding the more precise explanation of this phenomenon. I want to consider Klein's, which I find convincing. Klein argues that in this rare case we find the painfulness itself pleasant. This calls for explanation. Klein's explanation is that masochistic pleasures have a unique quality that he calls 'penumbrality.' Masochistic pleasures are just on the edge of what we can bear. In the case of the loose tooth, Klein comments:

> That is why one finds a certain *fascination* at work in these cases. People don't push a loose tooth once and then stop. They keep returning, pushing right to the edge of what they can bear, and then backing off, sometimes going over, and in general making exploratory sallies right around the borderline where the sensation becomes too much.
>
> (48)

Furthermore, as Klein notes, this kind of explanation handles cases of sexual masochism very well. The practice of masochism often involves explicitly finding and locating the edges – one enjoys the nearness of extreme danger, but when playing with fire there are important limits to recognize.

Notice that penumbrality is essentially a meta-evaluative property. It depends upon an explicit or implicit assessment of nearby sets of experiences, and of the location of one's present experience with respect to those sets. Penumbrality, I would say, depends upon salient properties of one's experience bearing relations to other, usually less salient properties, such as one's expectations or imagistic presentations regarding how things might otherwise go.

One reason to discuss the role of meta-evaluative properties in consciousness is simply to chart one interesting feature of our experiences in virtue of which they bear non-derivative value. A second reason is that this feature is a problem for overly simple hedonistic models. I have claimed that a thick experience E bears value in virtue of the properties that make E what it is. These include the determinate non-evaluative properties that give an experience its shape. According to the considerations advanced in this chapter, meta-evaluative properties will sometimes – perhaps often in humans – play a role as well.

One might insist nonetheless that an experience bears value only in virtue of its evaluative and meta-evaluative properties. But this strikes me as a very unnatural position to take. Meta-evaluative properties depend essentially on the more determinate properties of the experience, as well as an experience's place in an implicitly understood map of surrounding experiences. This is why it is so natural to cite the more determinate properties in explanations of the value of the experience. Why was the experience of chewing the betel nut valuable? In part, because one had never experienced that particular kind of buzz before.

I am at risk of belaboring the point. But I want to close this chapter by illustrating the way that an experience's complexity, where that includes a range of phenomenal property-types, may play a role in helping us understand why an experience bears the type and amount of value that it does. I do so via a deep dive into an interesting bit of phenomenology due to Uriah Kriegel (2015).

Kriegel offers a phenomenological analysis of a very unique experience of *freedom*. The experience is his own, and occurred earlier in his life, upon release from prison. (Kriegel did time for good moral reasons.) I cannot do justice to Kriegel's reconstruction of the experience – it takes Kriegel several pages – but I wish to discuss elements of it nonetheless. Kriegel identifies a number of distinct elements within the experience, which he describes as lasting approximately five hours. I'll mention ten of them.

First, Kriegel's experience involved a feeling of being uncompelled. 'It was very vivid before my mind that nobody could tell me what to do, that there was nothing I needed to do or could be required to do' (215). Second, Kriegel felt unconstrained: he felt that no external force could prevent him from doing whatever he wanted. Kriegel notes that

> An interesting feature of both feelings was that they were felt as boundless, virtually all-encompassing: I had the feeling that I could do (or avoid doing) anything – if I only wanted to . . . The feeling was . . . that actions in general were open to me
>
> (216)

Third, Kriegel's experience had an element of rightness. 'It felt right to be where I was, doing what I was doing, being who I was . . . [this] was in vivid evidence during large tracts of those five hours' (216).

Fourth, Kriegel's experience included a very positive, determinate sort of valence. Kriegel describes it as

> an unusual kind of elation or euphoria, distinguished by the lack of that energetic, enthusiastic, adrenalined strand in more common moments of euphoria. I would describe it as a sort of passive bliss. I was very alert, very aware, and things were felt with great clarity and acuity – as they can under the influence of certain stimulants – but I was not overtaken by any energy that needed to find its outlet, and as mentioned there was nothing in particular I felt like doing. It just felt good.
>
> (217)

Fifth, Kriegel felt an absence of anxiety that he calls a phenomenology of 'extraordinary calm' (217). Sixth, Kriegel reports he experienced greater perceptual acuity. Seventh, Kriegel's point of visual focus was changed:

> Whereas on a regular day the space five to twenty-five yards straight ahead of me commands my visual attention, on that day the point of attraction lay about forty to sixty yards ahead and slightly to one side or the other. My gaze was somehow lifted, removed from the immediate surroundings. (Perhaps this had to do with a general sense of being removed from the world.)
>
> (218)

Eighth, Kriegel's attention was much more drawn to natural features of his environment. Ninth, 'the relative proportion of ongoing self-awareness and world-awareness in my overall awareness was persistently balanced' (218).

Tenth, Kriegel remarks on temporal elements to this experience.

> It had a rhythm not unlike other powerful prolonged experiences. What I describe above is based on the episode's peaks of phenomenal intensity, which recurred in intervals of twenty to thirty minutes (though my memory here feels uncertain). There were also ebbs in which the described phenomenology was less clear and distinct – though at no time did I feel quite as one does in the ordinary go of things. The phenomenological extraordinariness was stubborn. Perhaps the most powerful peak in the entire episode marked itself in my memory with great overall precision, of the sort that characterizes traumas or turning points in one's life (see under: "Where were you on 9/11?").
>
> (218)

Finally, Kriegel notes an interesting interaction between the nature of the experience and the direction of his attention on its nature.

> On a number of occasions, I became focally and reflectively aware of the very extraordinariness of the overall experience I was undergoing.

> Like a headache slowly becoming so painful as to command one's focal attention, the phenomenal intensity of what I was experiencing occasionally became so overwhelming that it involuntarily attracted my attention. Unfortunately, it was impossible to dwell on it overmuch: the phenomenology appeared to blur under introspective microspection. It could only flourish, apparently, in the state of the right balance between world-awareness and self-awareness. Eventually, the phenomenology started slowly dissipating, in something that was experienced as painful loss, not unlike the way one feels when the state of bewitchment following a powerful film – the feeling that says "From now on that is how I am going to live my life!" – starts to dissipate, leaving behind it only the oppressive banality of the present.
>
> (218–219)

I quote Kriegel at such length in part because this was his experience, and in part because paraphrase wouldn't allow the point I wish to make to come through with enough vividness. The point is this: clearly this experience seems, in Kriegel's view, to bear a lot of value. Speaking personally, I can think of one or two times in my life where I had an experience similar in some ways. I consider these amongst the most valuable experiences of my life – and the value the experience bears depends in clear ways on related elements of what is best considered a very thick, very complex experience. Some of these elements are evaluative, some are meta-evaluative, and some are descriptive. It is not at all clear these can be disentangled in any way friendly to the hedonist. But even if they could, it borders on absurdity to think that the *overall shape* of the experience is not central to any explanation of its status as a highly valuable experience. The experience is highly valuable in virtue of its shape, and not simply in virtue of the hedonic properties present therein.

13 Evaluative spaces, part I

> I have sought love, first, because it brings ecstasy – ecstasy so great that I would often have sacrificed all the rest of this life for a few hours of this joy.
> (Bertrand Russell)

One attractive feature of [Hedonism About Phenomenal Value] is that it makes it relatively easy to imagine how comparisons of phenomenal value ought to go. One simply tots up the positivity or negativity inherent in an experience or collection of experiences, and one assumes a straightforward function from valence to value. I have argued that while this model seems to capture some valuable experiences, the full picture must be more complex than this. That leaves us with a problem: if phenomenal value cannot be easily conceptualized in terms of cleanly constructed quantities, how are we supposed to conceptualize preferences regarding items with phenomenal value? And how are we to think about, or attempt to resolve, difficult cases involving comparison and conflict between items with phenomenal value?

Let us split the general problem into two. One part of this problem has to do with phenomenal value within a single entity – someone like you or me stretched out over time. A second part has to do with value comparisons between different kinds of entity. Let us take the first part first.

Suppose that by the time your long life is close to its natural end technology has advanced enough to allow uploading. This is a procedure that enables you to upload into a kind of matrix many of your memories and skills, as well as a psychological control center modeled after your own mind. Of course you are uncertain whether this uploaded thing will really be *you*, but you figure it is close enough that you ought to take the procedure seriously. You spring for a business class version of uploading. So you are instructed to indicate, in the form of an ordering, the best kinds of experiences. These will be weighted appropriately, and your upload will be placed in a virtual environment that enables systematic access to these kinds of experiences, given the constraints provided by your own memories, skills, and mind-model. (Spring for first-class uploading, and you can tweak your skills. But this is expensive, and the worries about whether this will really be you will then be amplified.) You are allowed some latitude in how you define an *experience* – certain temporally extended patterns qualify. What kind of ordering do you produce, and why?

If you are thinking about phenomenal value in the way that I am, you probably do not think straightforwardly in terms of the most positive or negative experiences. Rather, you attend to the overall shape of various types of experience. In so doing it is possible to place some kinds of experiences towards the top and some kinds towards the bottom.[1] Let us focus on those. Why are they located towards the top or bottom? My answer to this question runs through a notion I need to introduce. I think the phenomenal value our experiences bear is explained in part in terms of the location of these experiences within a (more or less) sophisticated *evaluative space*.

All humans, and all entities we would consider conscious in anything like the way that we are conscious, possess an evaluative space. To attribute an evaluative space to an entity is in part to say that it is disposed to consciously evaluate exterior and interior objects and events – not necessarily to form explicit judgments about these objects and events, although such judgments will be part of the story for humans. But primarily I am speaking here of the tokening of evaluative conscious mental states and processes of various sorts in response to incoming stimuli. Our evaluations may come in various sorts. Some will come in the form of fleeting desires. One day you may evaluate a jam doughnut as to-be-eaten-immediately; the next day you may evaluate it as fatty and disgusting. Some evaluations are more stable, and organized around particular items. Our cares take this shape – cares, as philosophers sometimes explicate them (Jaworska 2007), are stable and more or less complex patterns of evaluative responding to items of attachment, e.g., the pattern associated with your cherished pet. Some evaluations are largely implicit. Think, for example, of the strong emotions sometimes associated with the beginning stages of attraction to another person. The emotions may be volatile and powerful even if one has no understanding of why one evaluates the other person in that way. By contrast, some evaluations are largely explicit. One might rate Elizabeth Camp's article 'Putting Thoughts to Work' as one of the finest and most insightful articles to emerge from the philosophy of mind in the twenty-first century, and one might do so for multiple reasons one could explicitly articulate and defend against a disagreeing philistine. All of the evaluative states one tokens are ways of expressing elements of one's evaluative space. Of course, for adult humans, the space is fairly complex, and one's fleeting, stable, implicit, and explicit evaluations often interact and intermingle.

This notion of an evaluative space is important for how we might think about comparisons of phenomenal value within a single entity. It does not explain why some of one's experiences bear more phenomenal value than others. Rather, it depends on the fact that some of one's experiences do bear more value than others. The notion of an evaluative space is useful simply for purposes of conceptualizing differences of value between experiences. In general, experiences that involve experiential assessment of items, objects, and events that one (implicitly or explicitly) finds highly significant, highly meaningful, or in some other way important, significant or good will tend to be more valuable – or disvaluable, depending on the relationship between the item and one's assessment in the context of one's own evaluative space.[2]

Regarding this claim, it may be illuminating to note a connection with Wayne Sumner's theory of happiness (Sumner 1996). Sumnerian happiness is embedded in a sophisticated theory of well-being. For Sumner, well-being is authentic happiness: happiness that is an evaluation that is genuinely or freely made (i.e., that is autonomous in some sense), and that is based on good information (i.e., that is accurately directed at one's actual life). The authenticity requirement is meant to rule out certain counter-examples involving well-being, and is not my reason for discussing Sumner. It is only Sumner's account of happiness that I want to discuss.

For Sumner, happiness is not just pleasure or enjoyable experience. Rather, the meaning we attach to experience is critical (141). Sumner distinguishes the experiences constitutive of happiness from three related kinds of experience. The first kind Sumner calls 'being happy with or about something' (143). This kind of happiness simply involves one's possessing a favorable attitude towards some intentional object. The second kind of happiness is 'feeling happy' (144). This kind involves feeling something – what Sumner describes as a kind of mood or cheer or euphoria, which is attended by a sense of completeness and peace (144). The third kind of happiness is a settled tendency or disposition to experience positive moods (145). The final kind of experience is the crucial one – it is 'that in which you are (have been) happy or your life is (has been) a happy one' (145).

This central kind of happiness has a cognitive and an affective component. The cognitive component is, like the first kind of happiness, the possession of a favorable attitude. The difference is the range of relevant intentional objects – the favorable attitude in question is directed at the conditions of your life, which may include your life as a whole, or may (at minimum, it seems) include one of the 'important sectors of your life' (145), e.g., your work or your family. The affective component 'consists in what we commonly call a sense of well-being: finding your life enriching or rewarding, or feeling satisfied or fulfilled by it' (146). Happiness, then, is a positive attitude towards one's life or important sectors of one's life, which is accompanied by a distinct feeling of satisfaction.

Sumner has his finger on an important kind of thick experience. It involves an assessment of something one tends to find highly significant or meaningful: one's own life. I think such experiences can be highly valuable or disvaluable, depending on how the assessment goes. I do not agree with Sumner that this one kind of experience could *on its own* function as the central determinant of happiness. But I do not want to offer my own account of happiness. I am stalking an account of phenomenal value, and I think Sumner's experience of assessing one's life is an excellent example of how certain regions within one's evaluative space can produce experiences of great value or disvalue.

One reason why is that our evaluative experiences are clearly influenced by what Cain Todd has called 'subjective evaluative conditions': conditions such as a subject's 'various motivations, interests, beliefs, goals, cares, values, character traits, imaginative and attentive capacities, other psychological characteristics, and even physical constitution' (2014, 97). These conditions are wide-reaching, involving elements of one's cognitive systems, but additionally including elements that directly impact one's experiential capacities. For entities with similar minds and bodies, the latter elements will be similar to each other, although there will still be individual differences. Some individuals have heightened sensory capacities. Others seem to be able to empathize or to feel certain emotions more deeply. Such differences may extend an individual's evaluative space beyond another's in certain ways, and may thereby enable more valuable and disvaluable experiences along certain dimensions.

In earlier chapters I have indicated one feature that may influence the amount and type of value borne, namely, the complexity of the experience. The function of this notion of an evaluative space is to deepen the explanation somewhat. Complexity on its own is not that important: a complex experience may be distracting or anxiety-inducing or simply boring. But a complex experience may put items into relationships that render the experience valuable in certain ways: highly enjoyable, deeply meaningful, very interesting, or whatever. The suggestion I offer here is that an experience's capacity to do so will generally track the location of the relevant items and relationships within a subject's particular evaluative space.

Note, incidentally, that the claim is not that a subject's values or cares have to be correct or appropriate in some sense. The claim is that the value a subject's experience bears has to do with features of its phenomenal character that are explained by the subject's own values and evaluative capacities – by a relationship between the experience and the subject's broader evaluative space.

To say this much is to fall far short of anything like an account of the features in virtue of which one's experiences bear more or less value. In some systems, a good biological or evolutionary account of the system's evaluative capacities will do a lot of this work. In systems as complex as human beings, biology may do some work, but perhaps not all of it. David Wiggins (1987) notes that though we often classify items as pleasing or annoying or whatever 'precisely *because* they are such as to please, help, amuse us . . . or harm, annoy, vex us . . . in their various ways' (195), these classifications admit of changes, refinements, and perhaps even improvements.[3] Consider why we classify items as *funny*. Perhaps because such items provoke amusement. But, Wiggins notes,

> one person can improve another's grasp of the concept of the funny; and one person can improve another's focus or discrimination of what *is* funny . . . the process can be a collaborative one, without either of the participants to a dialogue counting as the absolutely better judge. The test of improvement in this process of mutual instruction and improvement can be at least partially internal to the perceptions of its participants.
>
> (196)

Our evaluative systems and capacities are complex, and we often exercise some element of creativity and exploration in refining the evaluative space we possess. Wiggins claims that through this process of refinement, we may not only change our evaluations, but improve them in the sense that we 'get more and more cognitive-cum-affective satisfaction' out of the evaluations that we make.

One upshot is that the evaluative space a human possesses is not fixed in a crude way; we have a sense of its malleability, and this gives impetus to the way we instruct children, and engage in dialogue and debate about what (items of) experiences are valuable. Such malleability also leaves room for surprise: experience teaches that we can sometimes be surprised by the things that mean the most to us. Even so, there is room here for a more substantive phenomenology of value – for the fact is that many of us do find certain items and patterns of activity experientially valuable, and we can instruct others in the best ways to discover the value for themselves. A substantive phenomenology of value would map out some of the stable patterns that are available to beings with subjective evaluative conditions such as ours.

To repeat, then, I do not here aim to offer an account of the specific features in virtue of which our experiences bear more or less value. My aim here is simply to indicate one fruitful way to conceive of differences in the value that one's different experiences bear. It seems there is an interesting correlation, at the very least, between experiences associated with certain items (events, states of affairs, objects, people, one's own body), the place of these items within a broad evaluative space, and the shape the relevant experiences tend to take. What one ought to prefer are experiences associated with items one assesses in explicit and implicit ways as highly valuable, where these experiences engage one's central evaluative capacities.

Notes

1 There may very well be differences in comparability between different kinds of experience. Watching my kids open Christmas presents is great (provided they don't act spoiled in so doing). So is the feeling of getting off the bus in London and knowing I have a whole day to myself. So is the feeling one gets after one beer. So is the very mixed but powerful surge of emotion evoked by the scene in *Eternal Sunshine of the Spotless Mind* that has the two principal characters sitting on the beach, realizing that their relationship and all memories associated with it is about to be erased. Insert your own set of experiences here. The experiences all seem to bear phenomenal value, although they are different in ways that makes them difficult to compare. For discussion of how to think about rational deliberation and choice in conditions of value incommensurability, see (Hsieh 2016).

2 For at least two reasons, this need not entail that in constructing a life, one ought only to focus on experiences connected with what one regards as the most meaningful or significant items. First, focusing only on experiences within certain regions of evaluative space – neglecting the simple pleasures, for example – might give one's life a kind of experiential imbalance. Second, such a focus may be biologically unrealistic. Even so, a defeasible rule in favor of pursuing items of great value as opposed to the simple pleasures seems to constitute good advice.

3 Thanks to Roger Crisp for making the connection between my thought here and Wiggins's.

14 Evaluative spaces, part II

> He woke all night with the cold. He'd rise and mend back the fire and she [that is, a wolf] was always watching him. When the flames came up her eyes burned out there like gatelamps to another world. A world burning on the shore of an unknowable void. A world construed out of blood and blood's alkahest and blood in its core and in its integument because it was that nothing save blood had power to resonate against that void which threatened hourly to devour it.
>
> (Cormac McCarthy)

> A fly or a maggot in its proper haunts, is as happy as a hero or patriot or friend, who has newly delivered his country or friend, and is surrounded by their grateful praises.
>
> (Francis Hutcheson)

As these passages forewarn, we've come to a difficult place. It seems comparisons between the phenomenal value born by different kinds of entities are necessary. But it is not at all clear how to go about making the comparisons. Different kinds of entities will potentially have mental lives and conscious experiences with structures and shapes vastly different from ours. So there is a genuine epistemological difficulty confronting any attempt to compare phenomenal value across such chasms.

In light of it, I think the best thing to do is to take courage and proceed, but with extreme epistemological humility. The considerations I offer in this chapter, therefore, must remain tentative, meager, and abstract.

I think the notion of an evaluative space can be of use here as well. When thinking about the evaluative space of an entity with a mind different from ours, however, appealing to intuitive and shared notions like one's cares and values may not generate as much traction. We must pay closer attention to the differences that shape an entity's evaluative space.

Consider two ways of abstractly characterizing the space. First, we might characterize an evaluative space in terms of the number, type, and subtlety of a subject's affective-evaluative capacities, where these are the capacities most directly relevant to the affective-evaluative properties of the entity's experiences. Call a characterization in terms of the number, type, and subtlety of these capacities a characterization of the *size* of an evaluative space. To illustrate, compare two entities, each with four evaluation-relevant capacities. It doesn't matter what they are, but say they involve touch, vision, audition, and emotion. Compared to Entity B, Entity A has very subtle versions of these capacities. This may be because A's perceptual capacities are much more subtle, or because the emotional capacities that enable A to evaluate the deliverances of perception are much more subtle, or both. The upshot is that the number and range of evaluative properties A's experience attributes to the world far outstrip those of Entity B. In this sense, Entity A's evaluative space is bigger. Now compare Entity A with Entity X, which has eight evaluation-relevant capacities – those Entity A has plus olfaction, thermoception, electroreception, and nociception. In one sense, X's evaluative space is bigger than A's. X has more affective-evaluative capacities. But we can imagine that X's capacities are comparatively simplistic. The evaluations they are capable of producing have a rougher grain, or less subtlety. On this dimension, A's evaluative space is bigger. So A might have a bigger evaluative space along one dimension but not another.

Does a bigger space relate to phenomenal value in any interesting way? I think there is a general relationship. A bigger space along various dimensions seems to be associated with a greater potentiality for phenomenal value or disvalue.

Compare, for example, the experiences of a world-class composer or music critic with those of a small child when hearing a Debussy étude. Suppose both find the music pleasant. Both may be emotionally moved by the music. Even so, in virtue of their highly refined capacities for evaluating and experiencing music, it seems plausible to say that the composer or critic has the potential to token more valuable experiences than the child. This is because the music expert's relevant affective-evaluative capacities are far more subtle.

But now consider experiences associated with play. Our composer enjoys a good game of squash, and rightly values the associated experiences of (as William James put it) 'doing and daring' with his body. The child enjoys a good game of tag (what British children call 'It') on the playground. To watch the child go, one would have to guess that her experiences of play are at least as valuable as, and probably much better than, the composer's. Perhaps this has to do with the purity of the child's joy. Her affective-evaluative capacities are fully engaged in the play, leading to more absorbing, vivid experiences of fun. Or perhaps it has to do with the state of her body – unlike the composer, she is not ravaged by age and a sedentary lifestyle. Here I'm reaching back as best I can to my own childhood. To be honest, many of the experiences I seem to remember are far better than those I can manage these days. While I have an increased capacity to token value with respect to certain experiences, I seem to have a diminished capacity with respect to other experiences.

A second characterization[1] of the evaluative space focuses on interactions between various affective-evaluative capacities and other elements of an entity's mental life. I have in mind here an entity's capacities for memory, for reasoning, and for developing stores of knowledge regarding the world that gives that entity's experiences much of their content. Capacities such as these afford connections between areas of an entity's evaluative space. They allow expectation, prediction, and learning of various sorts to add depth and nuance to an entity's ongoing stream of consciousness. They connect experiences that might otherwise remain separate. We can call this a characterization of the evaluative space's *internal coherence*.

Prima facie, the more internally coherent an entity's evaluative space, the more complex and coherent that entity's experiences will be. Consider interocular transfer of learning. This involves extracting information presented to one eye for some learning purpose, and then demonstrating that whatever is learned generalizes to the extent that when the information is presented to the other eye, the subject displays understanding. Although some animals (e.g., horses: see Hanggi 1999) are quite good at this, some animals (e.g., rabbits [van Hof 1970] and pidgeons [Graves and Goodale 1977]) are pretty bad. In a classic article on animal consciousness, Daniel Dennett draws an interesting inference from this result.

> [I]f you train a rabbit that a particular shape is a source of danger by demonstrations carefully restricted to its left eye, the rabbit will exhibit no "knowledge" about that shape, no fear or flight behavior, when the menacing shape is presented to its right eye. When we ask what it is like to be that rabbit, it appears that at the very least we must put a subscript, dexter or sinister, on our question in order to make it well-formed.
>
> (1995, 701)

Dennett's subscript comment (*dexter* is Latin for right and *sinister* Latin for left) indicates his view: there is nothing it is like to be a rabbit, even if there may be something it is like for the right or left side of the rabbit's visual capacities. But Dennett is fairly dismissive of this latter possibility, commenting that 'The underlying presumption that Nagel's 'what is it like' question makes sense at all . . . is challenged by such possibilities' (1995, 702).

I mention interocular transfer of learning merely to illustrate that one's evaluative space may be more or less coherent and sophisticated depending on the degree to which one's cognitive capacities collaborate with one's affective-evaluative capacities to produce unified representational states and experiences, and unified patterns of thought and behavior. It is largely an empirical matter just how internally coherent an entity's evaluative space is. But it is very plausible that, at least up to a threshold point, the more internally coherent an entity's evaluative space, the more that entity will possess the potential for tokening highly valuable experiences.

Consider, for example, Alan Goldman's interesting theory of the value of aesthetic experience. According to Goldman, aesthetic experience simultaneously engages a range of cognitive and evaluative capacities. And it is in part the fact that these capacities seem to work together to present aesthetic items in coherent ways that renders the experiences so seemingly valuable. Goldman comments:

> I have characterized [aesthetic] experience in terms of the simultaneous challenge and engagement of all our mental capacities – perceptual, cognitive, affective, imaginative, even volitional – in appreciation of the relations among aspects and elements of artworks. Such engagement creates a rich and intense mental experience imbued with meanings from all these faculties operating in tandem and informing one another. The resultant experience closes the distance between the person who has the experience and the work of art, which becomes no longer just one object in an external world, but for a time the person's world itself, the world of his or her fully absorbed experience.
>
> (2006, 334)

We need not endorse any particular theory of aesthetic experience as such to draw important morals from Goldman's view. Fully engaged aesthetic experience is among the most valuable experience available to human beings. It appears that such experience is made possible in part by the features in virtue of which our evaluative spaces have considerable size as well as considerable internal coherence.

We should of course expect that the size and internal coherence of an evaluative space can come apart depending on the minded entity under consideration. Some entities may have enormous evaluative spaces with very little internal coherence – and the opposite may be true. We should also expect that in many entities size and internal coherence will interact. Given the manifest contributions of memory, learning, reasoning, and so on to many of our thick experiences, it is plausible that an entity with a high level of internal coherence may thereby enjoy a larger evaluative space.

What we are left with is a fairly complicated, multi-dimensional model of the evaluative space. Given the role I think the evaluative space plays in explaining why some experiences bear much (dis)value while others do not, this has ramifications for how we think about comparisons of phenomenal value. To be more specific, it may very well be that the space of phenomenal value is itself multi-dimensional – not reducible to amounts conceptualized as falling on the valuable or disvaluable end of a uni-dimensional scale.

How would this be relevant to comparisons of phenomenal value? By analogy, consider how to compare these works of art in terms of *amounts of beauty*: Paul Klee's painting 'Dogmatic Composition 1918,' Czeslaw Milosz's poem 'Artificer,' John Doubleday's sculpture 'Maurice Bowra,' and ANONHI's song 'Drone Bomb Me.' Can it be done? Certainly not in any straightforward way. For (I assert) the beauty contained by different kinds of artwork is multi-dimensional, and the works of art listed do not overlap in every dimension. If phenomenal value is like this, direct comparisons between entities with very different minds will rarely be appropriate. Instead one ought to attempt to properly conceptualize the relevant dimensions in play, and to articulate the value of an experience or set of experiences in terms of value along these dimensions.

This is no easy task, of course. But remember the warning from Chapter 3. We ought to avoid reducing reflection on value and valuing practices to a simple contest between simply construed amounts of value and injunctions to maximize or otherwise optimize the simply construed amounts. What we ought to want from moral philosophy is some measure of insight and guidance, and little in the way of false advertising or the misleading pretense that the whole truth has been captured. Does what I have said so far offer any measure of insight and guidance regarding the problem cases that motivated this book? I comment on this in the following chapters.

Note

1 A third way of thinking about the space makes reference to peaks and valleys. What the hedonists call 'intensity' or what we might call 'power' in an experience. Experiences of great awe might be an example, or Kriegel's experience of freedom. One might be able to capture much of this kind of thing in terms of size and internal coherence. But perhaps it is conceivable that an entity with a relatively simple evaluative space could nonetheless have experience with very high peaks and very deep valleys.

15 How far we have come

It is time to bring this book's second part to a close. I have attempted to develop an account of the non-derivative value within consciousness – an account of phenomenal value. The central claims for which I have argued are these:

The affective-evaluative claim. It is necessary and sufficient for the presence of some non-derivative value in a conscious experience that the experience has evaluative phenomenal properties that essentially contain affective phenomenal properties.

The strong evaluative claim. It is necessary and sufficient for the presence of some non-derivative value in a subject's mental life that the mental life contain episodes with essentially affective evaluative phenomenal properties.

The claim that evaluative experiences can, on their own, constitute items of great value.

The claim that what I called [Hedonism About Phenomenal Value] seems to capture the way some experiences bear value, but it cannot be the complete account of how experiences do so. Recall how I articulated this view:

> [Hedonism About Phenomenal Value] In a particular way, phenomenal value inherits its structure from the valence of phenomenal character. The more positive an experience's phenomenal character, the more value the experience bears. The more negative an experience's phenomenal character, the less value (or the more disvalue) the experience bears.

I gave a few reasons to think this view falls short of a full account of the relationship between phenomenal character and phenomenal value. First, it is unclear whether this view gets the phenomenology right. It may be an oversimplification of the phenomenal character of evaluative experiences to divide experiences into more and less positive and negative. Second, this view runs into trouble in any case when attempting to explain the way experiences bear value. In particular, this view is not naturally combined with a claim I defended regarding the way thick experiences – experiences that essentially contain evaluative and non-evaluative phenomenal properties – bear value. I argued that a thick experience E bears value in virtue of the properties that make E what it is. So an experience bears value not simply in virtue of its evaluative properties, but also in virtue of its overall shape.

Regarding comparisons of an experience's value, I introduced the notion of an evaluative space. I argued that regarding intra-personal comparisons of value, an interesting correlation exists between experiences associated with certain items (events, states of affairs, objects, people, one's own body), the place of these items within a broad evaluative space, and the shape the relevant experiences tend to take. What one ought to prefer are experiences associated with items one assesses in explicit and implicit ways as highly valuable, where these experiences engage one's central affective-evaluative capacities.

Regarding inter-entity comparisons of value, I again appealed to the notion of an evaluative space. I characterized an entity's evaluative space in terms of two interacting measures: the space's size and its internal coherence. I suggested that along certain dimensions, increases in size and in internal coherence increase an entity's potential for tokening valuable and disvaluable experiences.

In this book's short third part, I have the goal of *illustrating* how this account of phenomenal value can aid moral reflection on difficult cases. This is not a book that aims to solve these cases, or even to consider them at a sufficient level of detail and depth. This is a book motivated by these difficult cases, and by the thought that one dark region within our reflection on them concerns phenomenal value. It should be the case, then, that the account of phenomenal value helps. I think that it does, and the aim of the last three chapters is to indicate how.

I will not be attempting to derive any ingenious or sufficiently qualified moral principles out of the account. I do not think that principles are of much use when we turn to actual cases. What is of use is an understanding of the sorts of values and reasons at issue in a case, and an understanding of how the case shapes their particular instantiations. To offer an abstract preview, then, where I think the account of phenomenal value I have offered really helps is this: it directs attention away from some bad places, and towards some good places. This may seem minor, but in fact I think attending in the right ways is one of the very chambers of morality's heart.

Part III

Moral status and difficult cases

16 Moral status

Machines and post-persons

One large group of problem cases for commonsense morality revolves around the kinds of machines likely to emerge in the future. Some of the problems these cases raise have very little to do with the value present within consciousness. These are problems to do with the structure of society, the distribution of resources in economies that rely on highly functional machines, dangers to humans associated with an artificial intelligence explosion, and so on. That is not my focus here (but see Gunkel 2012; Bostrom and Yudkowsky 2014). My focus is on the value potentially present in the conscious mental lives of conscious machines, and how my account of phenomenal value might help us to reflect upon relevant potentialities.

Of course, broaching the possibility of conscious machines brings with it massive epistemological problems. How would we know that a machine is conscious? Because it tells us so? Because it mimics elements of human cognitive or perceptual functionality? How close must it mimic human functionality to warrant a verdict of conscious? Answers to this latter question must appeal to some theory of consciousness. But there are many competing theories, most of them designed in the first instance to explain certain features of adult human consciousness. Why think their insights, even if illuminating in the human case, transfer to the case of machines? These are all interesting questions, and in a different book it would be great fun to discuss potential answers at some length. Although it may be unsatisfying to some, however, I am going to assume that machines will someday emerge that are, in virtue of whatever features you like, at least potentially conscious. And I am going to conduct discussion conditionally: if we suppose these machines are conscious, how ought we to think about their moral status?

One salutary upshot of my view of phenomenal value is that it has the potential to reorient thinking regarding the moral status of sophisticated machines. In large part such thinking to date has been driven by speculation that such machines would be highly intelligent – perhaps much more intelligent than human beings – and that this intelligence gap generates moral problems.

It is crucial, in my view, to keep an eye on the difference between evaluative sophistication and domain-general intelligence, for many machines may incorporate very little in the way of an evaluative mental life. It really depends on what the machines are designed to do. Some such machines may be designed to mimic human functionality as closely as possible – perhaps using techniques of whole or part-brain emulation (Bostrom 2014). In that kind of case, there is good reason to think that the resultant entity would possess roughly the same potential for phenomenal value as a human. Given this, the kinds of purposes we might have for such an entity would need to be rigorously and publicly scrutinized.

In many cases, however, we might end up with machines that perform a range of tasks very well, and in that sense qualify as highly intelligent, even though the mental life of these machines contains very little in the way of evaluative sophistication. Bostrom considers a scenario.

> We could thus imagine, as an extreme case, a technologically highly advanced society, containing many complex structures, some of them far more intelligent than anything that exists on the planet today – a society which nevertheless lacks any type of being that is conscious or whose welfare has moral significance. In a sense, this would be an uninhabited society. It would be a society of economic miracles and technological awesomeness, with nobody there to benefit. A Disneyland without children.
>
> (2014, 173)

Recall the two characterizations I offered for an entity's evaluative space: size and internal coherence. It is plausible that for some particular entity's evaluative space, interactions between size and internal coherence will be important. One kind of interaction that seems relevant would be interactions between a system's chief goals and a system's general knowledge and uptake of information regarding the environment. There is a reason pain tends to be painful: we evolved to have goals in favor of the avoidance of bodily damage. Similarly, there are reasons (to do with goals involving reproduction, social status, and probably more) that we evaluate certain people as beautiful, and accordingly as very pleasant to behold, and as very rewarding to engage in conversation and whatever else. Whether *evaluative sophistication* emerges in a system may have to do with the relationship between that system's goals and the behavioral pathways to goal achievement necessitated by the system's architecture and environment. It is conceivable that some very smart systems would not need such sophistication – perhaps they will be able to achieve their goals in fairly simple ways. It is likewise conceivable that some systems will need considerable evaluative sophistication, even though the domain of evaluation is different from any about which you or I would care. A highly sophisticated machine created to design sturdy buildings for various purposes (aesthetic, functional, whatever) might possess remarkable sophistication related to the evaluation of physical materials, possible uses for construction, and so on. Perhaps such a machine could bear a high amount of phenomenal value as it set about evaluating some new environment for the purposes of designing a new structure. Conversely, a machine may have high levels of domain-specific intelligence, but a very small evaluative space. In terms of phenomenal value, then, even if such a machine were to qualify as conscious, they might be similar to a very simple animal.

Although there has been much recent speculation regarding pathways to an artificial intelligence explosion, there has been little reflection on the kinds of evaluative mental lives that might thereby be created. The account of phenomenal value here presented suggests that there is moral importance attached to this latter task.

Consider an influential article by Nicholas Agar in which he considers the possibility of supra-persons: persons of the future who have higher moral status than healthy adult human beings. According to Agar, the toughest problem for the proponent of the possibility of supra-persons has been articulated by Allen Buchanan (2009). It is, in short, that

> there seems a significant barrier in grasping the criteria that one must satisfy to be correctly pronounced a post-person. It is easy to imagine beings who are more intelligent than we are. But it is difficult to see how this greater intelligence could place them in a higher moral category.
>
> (Agar 2013, 69)

Agar responds to the difficulty in conceiving of the moral grounds for supra-personhood with an inductive argument. We ought to defer to more intelligent beings, and if they recognize beings with a higher status, we ought to believe them. Here Agar assumes those with higher status would be the more intelligent beings, although his argument cannot establish that. But it is clear he has in mind that it is in virtue of higher intelligence that the beings of the future would have higher moral status. As he puts it, 'Our deference to beings who lack our imaginative and intellectual limits resembles that which moderately talented students of mathematics grant to those whose mathematical skills are manifestly superior to our own' (70).

Would smarter beings recognize beings with higher moral status than us? Agar assumes an account of moral status on which adult humans have it because of their capacity for practical reasoning. And he claims that practical reasoning is more like mathematical knowledge and skill than it is like knowledge of language – that is, practical reasoning is infinitely improvable. Given that we grant some moral status to the 'merely sentient,' and that our enhanced powers of practical reasoning grant us higher moral status, we ought to think that beings with better reasoning powers than us would have even higher moral status.

I reject most aspects of this argument. In particular, I do not think that practical reasoning could be sufficient for moral status. If so, a smart machine trained on human decision-making variables and created solely to take my problems as input and output a decision about my best action-option would have a moral status similar to mine. I also think it is worth challenging the commonly held assumption that human beings have 'higher' moral status than many animals. These are all problems with the details of Agar's argument. My bigger problem is with the argument's overall orientation. The assumption is that it is *smarts* that matter for moral status. This fetishizes smarts, which are only derivatively valuable. What is more important, because it undergirds the non-derivative value available to an entity, is the nature of that entity's evaluative space.

Of course entities with higher moral status are still possible, and perhaps actual. The route my account of phenomenal value offers is through the phenomenal value available to the entity. It is plausible that certain enhancements to the size or the internal coherence of an evaluative space will significantly enhance the value of an entity's experiences. Whether such enhancements amount to 'higher' moral status will depend on one's view of moral status.

In this connection, recall the view of moral status I put forward in Chapter 4. On that view, talk of higher moral status is best understood as talk of the amount of non-derivative value available to an entity. But amounts are not the only relevant dimension to non-derivative value. I also emphasized the *particular* reasons to treat an entity in certain ways that arise from the *way* an entity bears non-derivative value. David DeGrazia invokes a similar idea when advancing an interesting model of moral status. DeGrazia calls it the Interests Model.

On this model, 'all sentient beings have interests and experiential welfare, possession of which is the sole basis for moral status' (2012a, 138). Even so, DeGrazia allows that there can be morally relevant differences between entities with the same level of moral status. For example, a principle of respect for autonomy applies to some beings and not others, because some beings have autonomy, and others do not. As DeGrazia notes,

> Paternalism is a serious moral issue where respect for autonomy conflicts with one or more consequentialist principles. It is not a serious issue when I prevent my young daughter from drinking alcohol, for her own good, or when I drag my dog to the vet, for his own good.
> (139)

DeGrazia maintains that differences in capacities and interests can justify differences in 'morally appropriate treatment,' even if levels of moral status do not differ.

Here is how I prefer to think about talk of levels of moral status, and of morally relevant differences that do not concern levels: talk of levels is talk at the limits of what we can do to an entity. Scenarios that involve killing the one for the many are relevant here. Many think killing a human is permissible only in extreme circumstances (although war or other international conflict counts as extreme for many people). Many think killing several mice is permissible so long as we are at least attempting to use them in a valid scientific experiment. One way to order entities with respect to levels of moral status is to consider which one ought to kill in scenarios that render the killing permissible while equalizing (so far as is possible) other morally relevant considerations. On the account of phenomenal value I have developed, what you ought to think about in such a scenario is not the entity's smarts, or whether it is rational, or self-aware. You ought to think about its evaluative sophistication, which I have argued is a function of the size and internal coherence of its evaluative space.

This does not entail that slight differences in phenomenal value will justify a choice of one entity over another. Many think that moral status is a *threshold* concept – once you reach a certain point, you have all the moral status there is to have. Others have suggested that moral status could increase in a non-linear way (Douglas 2013). I do not have a settled view. But it is worth noting that this talk of levels of moral status applies only in fairly extreme circumstances that involve killing or choosing some out of necessity (i.e. for the sake of others). It is possible that post-persons will emerge who have much more sophisticated evaluative spaces than we do, and that if it came down to a choice – us or them – it would make sense to us and them that they should be the ones to live.

17 Moral status

The other animals

A full consideration of the moral status of the other animals – the non-humans – is a life's project. Here my jurisdiction permits a very limited consideration of the ways my account of phenomenal value might help us reflect upon relevant questions. The areas I'm going to consider are two. First, there are questions about the harm we do to animals when we cause them to suffer, and about the benefit available to animals via valuable experiences. Second, there are questions about the harm (or benefit) we do to animals when we kill them. With respect to both areas, there are questions about value full-stop, and there are questions about comparison between, e.g., animal suffering and death and human suffering and death.

Before diving into these areas, I should at least say something about the difficult epistemological questions regarding what we know and do not know about the conscious lives of animals. These are questions about whether and how we could come to know that an animal's conscious mental life had a structure like thus-and-so. More detailed questions involve the specific kinds of experiences different species may have, whether such experiences have qualities that we would readily recognize – the involvement of attention, imagination, memory, sensory affect, emotion – and whether these experiences might be thought to be good or bad for the animal in ways we can understand. Such questions often prompt nuclear-grade skepticism and despair based upon the perception of a very high wall separating the third-personal methods of science and the essentially first-personal nature of consciousness. A lower grade of skepticism and despair might be associated with the perceived inadequacy of any current theory of consciousness to provide illumination regarding an animal's conscious mental life. I don't share the nuclear-grade skepticism, although I do think most current theories of consciousness – which have been developed to explain certain aspects of human consciousness – are not well-equipped to illuminate animal mentality. But as my account of phenomenal value is of no help regarding these epistemological questions, I will not pretend to have much to say. It is, however, important to note that we seem to have no substitute for paying close attention to the sciences of animal mentality. It seems an increasing number of writers in animal ethics understand this, and work very hard to relate relevant evidence to moral questions about animal quality of life. In my view the way forward is for animal ethics to become even more resolutely inter-disciplinary, and to recruit not only animal scientists, but philosophers of science, cognitive science, and neuroscience as well. For an example of what I have in mind here – an example that provides some rationale for avoiding nuclear-grade skepticism regarding knowledge of animal consciousness – see note 1.[1]

I turn to questions about the value and disvalue present within an animal's conscious experiences. Much of this will depend upon what evidence about animal mentality reveals. It is important to underline this: it should be evidence that guides us here. In spite of the way that some (not all) moral philosophers behave, this is not an area where a priori speculation should be given any weight. Fortunately, some moral philosophers take animal ethology seriously. David DeGrazia (2012b), Gary Varner (2012), Mark Rowlands (2012), and others have written empirically informed considerations of animal mentality and animal consciousness. I do not recapitulate their interesting and useful work here. Rather I restrict myself to some fairly abstract considerations to do with phenomenal value in animals.

Let us distinguish between the killing of animals, the use of animals in ways that cause suffering, and the use of animals in ways that do not cause suffering. I will be brief regarding the use of animals.

I take it that using animals in ways that cause suffering is to be avoided, and raises a question about how such use could be justified. How difficult it is to justify causing animal suffering will depend on the severity of the disvalue we thereby bring into being. In my view, we have to think through such cases in terms of the evaluative space of the relevant animal. That will require difficult empirical work, and difficult reflection on the relationship between relevant evidence and our best theories about the structure of the minds of certain kinds of animals. It is too cavalier to suggest, as many do, that because animals lack self-consciousness, or language, or 'rationality,' their mental lives contain less value than ours (for an argument against the moral significance of self-consciousness, see Shepherd 2017). On the account of phenomenal value I have developed, none of these features is necessary or sufficient for phenomenal value – although these features may serve as amplifiers of phenomenal value for some entities.

I think using animals in ways that do not cause suffering is morally permissible, provided we do not thereby block significant avenues to valuable experiences, and provided the actions that involve the use are not for other reasons impermissible. The non-derivative value present in an animal's conscious mental life is something to be protected and, if possible, facilitated. The way to protect and facilitate phenomenal value seems to depend, largely, on the kind of evaluative mental life at issue. Animals have goals and interests – what Bernard Rollin calls a *telos* (Rollin 1981) – and the frustration of these is generally bad for the animal. If it is possible to use the animal in ways that do not violate additional moral strictures, and that do not significantly frustrate these goals and interests, and if the animal lacks the capacity to conceptualize being used or to otherwise object to it, it seems nothing is amiss in so doing.

I turn to something our societies are very, very good at: killing animals. Why think killing an animal (human or non-human) is wrong? Philosophers have offered many subtly different accounts of the wrongness of killing, and of the importantly related ideas that death is bad and that death harms the person who dies. I cannot cover the gamut here. My discussion will focus on three accounts of the harm of death and of killing's wrongness, and the role phenomenal value might play in each.

The first account contains the following ideas. Death is bad, and harms the one who dies, because it deprives that being of access to non-derivative value. Killing is wrong, then, in virtue of the harm done to the one killed.[2]

The second account accepts that death is bad and a harm in virtue of deprivation – but it adds a cognitive layer. The harm of death is increased or decreased to the extent that the one killed would have been 'psychologically connected' to the future via 'prudential unity relations' – that is, interests in the goings on of one's future life that support psychological unity and continuity over time. Jeff McMahan calls these 'time-relative interests.' He offers several considerations in favor of the view that stronger time-relative interests render the killing of a human a much graver harm than the killing of a non-human. First, while a good may contribute more to a life's value 'to the extent that it has been and continues to be desired when it occurs' (2002, 197), the goods that occur in an animal's life 'tend to arrive unbidden and indeed unanticipated' (197). Second, while the psychological continuity of a human allows for a complex narrative structure that may enable a good to enhance the value of a life 'through its relations to earlier and later events within the life,' animals have 'no projects that require completion, mistakes that demand rectification, or personal relations that promise to ripen or mature' (198). Third, our long-range desires may take a long time to come to fruition, and consequently death may rob our activities in life of 'a meaning or value that was contingent upon future fulfillment' (198). Fourth, McMahan asserts that while the loss of goods that other conspecifics would have had is a bad thing for humans, it is not for animals: 'these comparative dimensions to the evaluation of death seem inapplicable or irrelevant in the case of animals' (198). Fifth, since 'there is, in the life of an animal, very little psychological architecture to be carried forward, and earlier and later mental states seldom refer to one another,' the 'goods in prospect' for an animal are 'comparatively meager' (198–199).

Although a number of McMahan's claims about the psychological lives of animals are empirical, he offers no evidence in support of them. Some of them may be true, although the literatures on comparative cognition and animal cognitive ethology suggest that for a great number of species the situation is far more complicated than McMahan intimates. But some – for example the claim about animals lacking psychological architecture to be carried forward, and the claim about goods occurring unbidden and unanticipated – are false (see the chapters in Zentall and Wasserman 2012). Even if we were to accept a time-relative interests account, then, it is not clear that the death of many animals would be such a meager harm.

But we should not accept a time-relative interests account.[3] It has been criticized from a number of different angles (see Liao 2007; Holtug 2011; Harman 2011; Bradley 2015). Ultimately, it gets the wrong results on a range of cases.[4] Consider, for example, the *Boltzmann Case*: a being with a fully functioning human-like nervous system spontaneously emerges thanks to random fluctuations in our universe, and remains functioning and stable for one day. This being's brain comes tuned with all the tunings of an adult human, such that it emerges with the full spate of memories and capacities. This person, then, goes about his day as though he were living an 80-year life. Would it be as wrong to kill this person as it is to kill any other? Yes. Or consider a case of *Radical Plasticity*: a human with a strange genetic mutation that allows for very rapid rewiring in the nervous system. This person picks up and loses new skills, languages, interests, hobbies, roughly every 10–12 months (you could make the timeframe whatever you like, of course). One side effect of the plasticity is that memories get overwritten, and if in the right external environments, the personality can change drastically from period to period. This person lacks the psychological unity that many higher animals seem to enjoy, although she has a sophisticated evaluative mental life. It is as wrong to kill her as it is to kill any other human.

A third kind of account is consistent with the claim that death harms in virtue of deprivation. But it finds an additional, and perhaps deeper, reason against killing. On this account, killing a conscious being with a certain level of evaluative sophistication violates the protections due such a being in virtue of the non-derivative value their life contains (in virtue of their experiential capacities). To illustrate, consider some remarks due to Jeff McMahan. Although McMahan endorses the time-relative interests account with respect to animals, he thinks humans call for an additional layer of protection, which he limns in this passage:

> The intuitive idea behind this view is that a person, a being of incalculable worth, demands the highest respect. To kill a person, in contravention of that person's own will, is an egregious failure of respect for the person and his worth. It is to annihilate that which is irreplaceable, to show contempt for that which demands reverence, to assert a spurious authority over one who alone has proper authority over his own life, and to assume a superior position vis-à-vis one who is in reality one's moral equal. Killing is, in short, an offence against what might be called a requirement of respect for persons and their worth. Indeed, because killing inflicts the ultimate loss – the obliteration of the person himself – and is both irreversible and uncompensable, it is no exaggeration to say that it constitutes the ultimate violation of the requirement of respect.
>
> (2002, 242)

McMahan thinks persons are of incalculable worth in virtue of some set of psychological capacities, although he remains agnostic on the precise nature of the capacities in the set save that they should differentiate humans from other animals. The account of killing's wrongness I am now considering dispenses with time-relative interests, and explains intuitions about incalculable worth in terms of an account of phenomenal value (rather than a stipulated set of psychological capacities).

Now, if we explain the worth of a being, and the protections due the being, in terms of the phenomenal value the being is capable of bearing, we have reason to question the assumption that only humans qualify. For the things often cited in favor of human specialness – language, self-consciousness – do not seem to be especially closely related to evaluative experiential capacities. It may be that humans have more phenomenal value available to them. But that is not immediately obvious.

I myself have some sympathy with a view articulated by William James in an 1899 essay "On a Certain Blindness in Human Beings." There James walks through many of the ways humans are prone to lose sight of the more fundamental experiential goods, and he expresses sympathy with the idea that these are goods to which not only humans have access.

> Living in the open air and on the ground, the lo-sided beam of the balance slowly rises to the level line; and the over-sensibilities and insensibilities even themselves out. The good of all artificial schemes and fevers fades and pales; and that of seeing, smelling, tasting, sleeping, and daring and doing with one's body, grows and grows. The savages

> and children of nature, to whom we deem ourselves so much superior, certainly are alive where we are often dead, along these lines; and, could they write as glibly as we do, they would read us impressive lectures on our impatience for improvement and on our blindness to the fundamental static goods of life.
>
> (1983, 146)

James concludes the essay with a plea for epistemic humility regarding the value of the lives of beings not like us: we ought not be 'forward in pronouncing on the meaninglessness of forms of existence other than our own.' Instead we ought to

> tolerate, and respect, and indulge those whom we see harmlessly interested and happy in their own ways, however unintelligible these may be to us. Hands off: neither the whole of truth nor the whole of good is revealed to any single observer.
>
> (146)

Adept readers will have noted that the account of harm I am discussing actually leaves open what animals ought to be accorded 'incalculable worth.' Earlier I articulated the wrongness of killing with respect to beings *with a certain level of evaluative sophistication*. It seems we cannot escape the philosopher's yen for line-drawing. And attempting to say just what levels of evaluative sophistication are morally relevant, or reach the appropriate threshold, or whatever, will of course pitch us into the thicket of difficulties associated with finding consistency regarding who should be in and who should be out. I have no special path through the thicket.

I do think, however, that the account of phenomenal value I have developed, in conjunction with an account of killing's wrongness that ties protections to phenomenal value, makes available a way around many of the difficulties. The cost would be a radical reformation of moral judgments and practices regarding the other animals. For the way around the thicket is to find incalculable worth in all but the simplest and dullest kinds of conscious mental life, and thus to draw the line quite low on the evolutionary totem pole. The upshot of this kind of view is its consistency, and its avoidance of the real moral risk associated with current moral judgments and practices (cf. DeGrazia 2014).

Notes

1 Andrew Barron and Colin Klein (2016) present an inductive case for insect consciousness. The case – necessarily oversimplified here – involves the following claims. First, evidence indicates that in vertebrates certain sub-cortical

midbrain structures are necessary and sufficient for consciousness. Second, on a number of functional measures, functionally analogous structures exist in the insect brain. These measures include running a behavioral core control system, enabling flexible action, and development of computational models of the surrounding environment that also place the animal itself into the environment in action-supporting ways. Given the functional similarities, Barron and Klein infer that the neural structures that support consciousness in vertebrates are likely possessed by insects as well.

2 For different ways of working out details of a deprivation account of the harm of death, see Feldman (1991), Broome (2012), and Bradley (2009). It is an additional but not terribly controversial step to claim that killing is wrong in virtue of the harm done. Proponents of such a view should, of course, remain cognizant that many additional factors can influence the wrongness of killing (see McMahan 2002, 189–265). As McMahan notes, these include 'the agent's motives, intentions, and mode of agency, side effects, whether the victim is responsible in a way that makes him liable to be killed, whether the agent is specially related to the victim, and so on' (2002, 194).

3 Indeed, in the end McMahan argues that the account 'is not a fully plausible general account of the morality of killing' (204), and adopts a further principle of (roughly) respect for beings with the psychological sophistication to qualify as 'persons.'

4 Some of these are discussed by McMahan (2015).

18 Moral status

Human cases

I am going to restrict myself to comments on two kinds of case. Both bring a number of additional moral complications into play – appealing to an account of phenomenal value will be of some assistance, but will certainly not answer every morally relevant question. To illustrate this I introduce the cases with brief descriptions.

Case one: traumatic brain injury

Say that a person, P, is injured in an accident, survives, and is diagnosed as being in a Minimally Conscious State (MCS). There is little chance for recovery out of MCS. P's partner, T, visits P frequently and notes some evidence of awareness of P's surroundings. P occasionally smiles, and occasionally indicates discomfort. Some in T's family ask whether T ought to press to have artificial nutrition and hydration removed. T is not willing to do so initially. This is because T and P had multiple conversations about just this kind of scenario, and P never indicated he would want to be allowed to die in such a condition. In fact, P indicated a kind of curiosity about the condition, once remarking: 'no one really knows what it's like to have such severe brain injuries. What if it's not bad at all? What if it's pretty good? Why end your life early if your life is going pretty well?' However, the more T visits P and speaks to doctors, the more she worries, and the more she begins to have doubts. Even if P's life is going 'pretty well' in some sense, it is clear that P and T's relationship has drastically changed. Indeed, it is no longer clear to T that P could be considered the same person he was. T begins to worry that P's life could be going well enough to justify continuing with physical therapy, medical treatment, and so on. T feels terrible about having such thoughts, and articulates them to no one. What T really wants to know is more about what it is like to be P in his current condition. What kinds of experiences is he able to have? Are there any that are very good, or any that are very bad? How could she contribute to giving him a better quality of life?

As the case of P and T illustrates, there are many morally relevant factors at issue in cases of traumatic brain injury (see Shepherd 2016b). There are questions about P's prior wishes. There are questions about what is in P's best interests now. There are questions about the value of prolonged life in P's condition. There are questions about how to improve P's life, and about how much improvement is actually possible. Not all of these questions directly implicate the phenomenal value present in P's life, but some do. And that may be important for how we think about the value of a life such as P's.

In this connection, the one point I wish to make regarding the case of P and T, and similar cases, involves how we think about the science of the traumatically injured brain.[1] In 2006 this science got an important jolt from a study published by Adrian Owen and colleagues (Owen et al. 2006). They showed that a patient previously diagnosed as in a Vegetative State – that is, a state lower on the functionality hierarchy than MCS – was able to respond to commands to imagine walking around rooms of the patient's house, and that this patient's brain behaved similarly to the brains of healthy adults when they imagined walking around the rooms of their houses. This study brought into the light the possibility that diagnoses of Vegetative State and MCS may miss significant retained mental function, highlighting just how little we still know about the traumatically injured brain.

One very sensible response to this study and follow-up studies has been to think hard about our diagnostic criteria, and about how we might make them more accurate. Another sensible response has been the attempt to develop methods for communicating with traumatically injured patients. Of course, given the nature of the injuries, in many cases communication is difficult, and in many more impossible. In a recent study utilizing behavioral measures and neuroimaging techniques, Osborne, Owen, and Fernández-Espejo (2015) report that only three out of sixty-eight patients were "able to successfully communicate accurate answers to yes/no questions in the scanner . . . while a fourth exhibited communication capabilities but failed to produce correct answers" (2).

An alternative response to the evidence of preserved functionality in those with traumatic brain injuries would be to study preserved evaluative capacities. Consider, for example, a recent study by Osborne and colleagues (2015). In one condition healthy participants were instructed to execute a movement or to imagine doing so. In another condition, they were allowed to voluntarily select the movement or the imagined movement. The voluntary condition was associated with significantly higher activation in regions associated with top-down motor control: pre-supplementary motor area and middle frontal gyrus. Osborne and colleagues apply this study to the case of the brain injured, arguing that detection of similar patterns of activation might serve as evidence that capacities enabling voluntary selection of activity are preserved.

What does this have to do with the retention of evaluative capacities? The capacity for voluntary selection is decomposable into important subcapacities, e.g., capacities to hold contents in working memory, to compare contents, and to initiate execution of a preferred action. This capacity in human adults seems to require evaluation of action options and associated consequences. As I have argued elsewhere, future research could extend this general strategy to examine evaluative capacities. One line of research that could help people such as T in our case would be research on responses to emotional stimuli. It turns out that researchers have provisionally attempted to assess residual emotional function in some patients. But no systematic attempt to assess levels of emotional functioning has been conducted (see Perrin, Castro, Tillmann, and Luauté 2015). As a result, although it is known that patients with traumatic brain injuries retain some capacity for functional response to emotional and self-relevant stimuli, the level or complexity of their emotional lives is not well understood. But it could be better understood – the thing to do is simply to study brain injured patients emotional assessments of stimuli, and to compare their capacities with those of healthy adults. This kind of work is already being done with respect to communicative capacities. If, as I have argued, the evaluative sophistication of a person's mental life is critical to the value present in that person's experiences, then there is a strong moral motivation to pursue this kind of research.

Case two: intellectual disability

Millat and Irie are a young couple living in East Oxford, in a nice terraced house just off the Cowley Road. After their doctor delivers some happy news – they're pregnant! – they find themselves inundated with NHS pamphlets and a wealth of passive-aggressive blog pieces about pregnancy. One of the pamphlets is pressed upon them with particular urgency by more than one health care professional. They get the message that it is important to voluntarily decide to get screenings for Down's, Edward's, and Patau's syndromes. Not wanting to be remiss, they do so. The screening for Down's syndrome returns a verdict of high risk. Millat's initial reaction is firm: they should terminate the pregnancy. Irie is unsure, however, and further research leaves her in a state of better-educated uncertainty. She shows some of this research to Millat, and he enters a state of deep uncertainty, and deep anxiety as well. There seem to be so many factors to weigh. What is the risk that the child will have a severe intellectual disability? What kinds of potential health problems might be associated with Down's syndrome?

What kind of financial burdens will Millat and Irie face? Are they up to the anticipated emotional burden? Would they develop a creeping resentment at the child or at each other over the decision not to terminate? Would they develop resentment, guilt, or regret over a decision to terminate? What kind of quality of life would the child have? Additional worries are associated with the timing of the screening. By the time the test result comes back, the fetus is eighteen weeks into development. Although UK law allows for late-term abortions if the fetus has Down's syndrome – this condition falls under 'Ground E,' which covers the risk of a child being born handicapped in some way – Irie is adamant that she will under no circumstances terminate the pregnancy if the fetus is older than twenty-four weeks. Although Millat rolls his eyes, Irie insists that beyond this point the fetus might become conscious, and that is the line Irie draws. That gives them precious little time to sort everything out.

As I hope this case illustrates, the decision facing Millat and Irie is extremely difficult and complex. I am focusing on their decision, but we could say the same thing about the policy background and medical practices that foreground their decision. There are a number of factors relevant to questions about how such screenings are presented and offered, about how we think about the decision to terminate a pregnancy, about the law surrounding late-term abortions and about exceptions made for conditions like Down's syndrome. In Millat and Irie's case, I have already discussed some of the relevant factors. The fetus's potential quality of life is but one of these. But it is nonetheless a very important one. It is undoubtedly the case that for some pregnant individuals or couples, the quality of life – and the quality of experiences that are so central to quality of life – functions as a trump card. If they came to believe that the fetus would have a high quality of life, they would bring it into the world. If they came to believe that the fetus would not, they would not. Whether that is an appropriate approach to such a difficult decision, I am not sure. I think there is something to be said for considering the existence of the individual at the very heart of matters.

What, then, should we say about quality of life for those with Down's syndrome? There is no one answer: the syndrome evinces a high degree of individual variability with respect to level of intellectual disability as well as susceptibility to physical and mental health challenges. In the main, Down's syndrome is associated with 'mild to severe' intellectual disability, as well as developmental delays and increased risk for psychological conditions like depression and Alzheimer's disease. Consider the association with intellectual disability and developmental delays. The latter represent a challenge, but it is not clear that on their own they represent a threat to quality of life. But one might worry about intellectual disability. In particular, one might think that the risk of even moderate intellectual disability is sufficient to downgrade the quality of life of such (prospective) individuals.

The account of phenomenal value I have offered, however, counsels otherwise. Certainly one's level of intellectual ability interacts with one's other abilities, and can contribute to the complexity and evaluative sophistication of one's experiences. But I have argued that the differences here are minimal when considered from the right altitude. What is far more important are well-functioning evaluative capacities – a robust emotional life, access to sensory pleasures, absence of chronic pain, and enough understanding of the world to develop sophisticated cares. Although cases involving severe intellectual disability are more difficult to adjudicate, and may represent significant detriments in terms of the quality of one's experiences, it seems to me that those with mild to moderate intellectual disability meet these conditions. In the case of individuals with Down's syndrome, one might learn this by speaking to one, or by reading or watching the readily available accounts of life with Down's syndrome. Emerging research further bolsters this judgment.

For example, children with Down's syndrome are not significantly different from other children at emotion recognition tasks (Pochon and Declercq 2013), and show similar developmental trajectories with respect to the acquisition of emotion knowledge (Channell, Conners, and Barth 2014). And a recent survey of health-related quality of life revealed that although children with Down's syndrome score lower than other children on measures of motor skill and cognitive development, they score the same on measures of physical complaints and measures of positive and negative emotions, and they score better (at least in this one survey) on a measure of anxiety and depression (van Gameren-Oosterom et al. 2011).

I do not think these kinds of results could or should determine one's assessment of Down's syndrome. But insofar as one's view of the reasons Millat and Irie have to weigh gives a central place to the quality of life of an individual who has Down's syndrome, I think it crucial to push past negative associations with and stereotypes of intellectual disability, and to consider the total conscious mental life of the individual in more detail. In many cases – those involving mild or moderate intellectual disability and lower risks of extreme health problems – individuals with Down's syndrome seem to have regular access to experiences that are just as valuable as any within the human range. If societal attitudes were to come to reflect that, and to reflect the idea that this is a more important fact than any fact about raw cognitive ability, the lives of those with Down's syndrome would likely improve even more.

Note

1 My reasoning here mirrors the reasoning deployed in Shepherd (2016a).

Bibliography

Agar, N. (2013). Why Is It Possible to Enhance Moral Status and Why Doing So Is Wrong? *Journal of Medical Ethics* 39(2): 67–74.

Baron, Marcia W. (1997). Kantian Ethics. In Baron, Marcia W., Pettit, Philip, and Slote, Michael. *Three Methods of Ethics: A Debate*. Hoboken, NJ: Wiley-Blackwell: 3–91.

Barron, Andrew B., and Klein, Colin (2016). What Insects Can Tell us About the Origins of Consciousness. *Proceedings of the National Academy of Sciences* 113(18): 4900–4908.

Bayne, Tim (2010). *The Unity of Consciousness*. Oxford: Oxford University Press.

Bennett, David, and Hill, Chris (eds.) (2014). *Sensory Integration and the Unity of Consciousness*. Cambridge, MA: MIT Press.

Bentham, Jeremy (1789). *An Introduction to the Principles of Morals and Legislation*. Pr. In 1780, and Now First Publ.

Bentham, Jeremy (1996). *An Introduction to the Principles of Morals and Legislation: The Collected Works of Jeremy Bentham*. Oxford: Oxford University Press.

Bostrom, Nick (2014). *Superintelligence: Paths, Dangers, Strategies*. Oxford: Oxford University Press.

Bostrom, Nick, and Yudkowsky, Eliezer (2014). The Ethics of Artificial Intelligence. In Keith Frankish and William R. Ramsey (eds.), *The Cambridge Handbook of Artificial Intelligence*. Cambridge: Cambridge University Press: 316–334.

Boyd, Brian (1993). *Vladimir Nabokov: The Russian Years*. Princeton, NJ: Princeton University Press.

Boyd, William (2009). *Any Human Heart*. London: Penguin Books.

Bradley, Ben (2009). *Well-Being and Death*. Oxford: Oxford University Press.

Bradley, Ben (2015). Is Death Bad for a Cow? In Tatjana Višak and Robert Garner (eds.), *The Ethics of Killing Animals*. Oxford: Oxford University Press.

Broome, John (2004). *Weighing Lives*. Oxford: Oxford University Press.

Broome, John (2012). The Badness of Death and the Goodness of Life. In Fred Feldman, Ben Bradley and Jens Johansson (eds.), *The Oxford Handbook of Philosophy and Death*. Oxford: Oxford University Press: 218–233.

Buchanan, Allen (2009). Moral Status and Human Enhancement. *Philosophy and Public Affairs* 37(4): 346–381.

Butchvarov, Panayot (1989). *Skepticism in Ethics*. Indianapolis, IN: Indiana University Press.

Chabon, Michael (2017). The True Meaning of Nostalgia. *New Yorker*, March 25, www.newyorker.com/books/page-turner/the-true-meaning-of-nostalgia.

Channell, Marie Moore, Conners, Frances A., and Barth, Joan M. (2014). Emotion Knowledge in Children and Adolescents With Down Syndrome: A New Methodological Approach. *American Journal on Intellectual and Developmental Disabilities* 119(5): 405–421.

Chisholm, Roderick M. (1975). The Intrinsic Value in Disjunctive States of Affairs. *Noûs* 9(3): 295–308.

Conder, Eustace Rogers (1877). *The Basis of Faith*. London: Hodder and Stoughton.

Crisp, Roger (2006). Hedonism Reconsidered. *Philosophy and Phenomenological Research* 73(3): 619–645.

DeGrazia, David (2008). Moral Status as a Matter of Degree? *Southern Journal of Philosophy* 46(2): 181–198.

DeGrazia, David (2012a). Genetic Enhancement, Post-persons and Moral Status: A Reply to Buchanan. *Journal of Medical Ethics* 38(3): 135–139.

DeGrazia, David (2012b). *Taking Animals Seriously: Mental Life and Moral Status*. Cambridge: Cambridge University Press.

DeGrazia, David (2014). On the Moral Status of Infants and the Cognitively Disabled: A Reply to Jaworska and Tannenbaum. *Ethics* 124(3): 543–556.

Dennett, Daniel C. (1991). *Consciousness Explained*. New York: Penguin Books.

Dennett, Daniel C. (1995). Animal Consciousness: What Matters and Why? *Social Research* 62: 691–710.

Deonna, Julien A., and Teroni, Fabrice (2011). *The Emotions: A Philosophical Introduction*. London: Routledge.

Deonna, Julien A., and Teroni, Fabrice (2015). Emotions as Attitudes. *Dialectica* 69(3): 293–311.

Didion, Joan (2005). *The Year of Magical Thinking*. London: Harper Perennial.

DiSilvestro, Russell (2010). Human Capacities and Moral Status. *Bioethics* 108: 165–199.

Dokic, Jérôme, and Lemaire, Stéphane (2013). Are Emotions Perceptions of Value? *Canadian Journal of Philosophy* 43(2): 227–247.

Dokic, Jérôme, and Lemaire, Stéphane (2015). Are Emotions Evaluative Modes? *Dialectica* 69(3): 271–292.

Dorsey, Dale (2010). Hutcheson's Deceptive Hedonism. *Journal of the History of Philosophy* 48(4): 445–467.

Douglas, Thomas (2013). Human Enhancement and Supra-personal Moral Status. *Philosophical Studies* 162(3): 473–497.

Ellis, Havelock (1898). Mescal: A New Artificial Paradise. *Contemporary Review*.

Feagin, Susan L. (1983). The Pleasures of Tragedy. *American Philosophical Quarterly* 20(1): 95–104.

Feldman, Fred (1991). Some Puzzles About the Evil of Death. *Philosophical Review* 100(2): 205–227.

Fish, William (2008). Relationalism and the Problems of Consciousness. *Teorema: International Journal of Philosophy* 28(3): 167–180.

Frijda, Nico H. (1987). Emotion, Cognitive Structure, and Action Tendency. *Cognition and Emotion* 1(2): 115–143.

Goldman, Alan H. (2006). The Experiential Account of Aesthetic Value. *Journal of Aesthetics and Art Criticism* 64(3): 333–342.

Graves, J.A., and Goodale, M.A. (1977). Failure of Interocular Transfer in the Pigeon (Columba Livia). *Physiology & Behavior* 19(3): 425–428.

Gunkel, David J. (2012). *The Machine Question: Critical Perspectives on Ai, Robots, and Ethics*. Cambridge, MA: MIT Press.

Hanggi, Evelyn B. (1999). Categorization Learning in Horses (Equus Caballus). *Journal of Comparative Psychology* 113(3): 243.

Harman, Elizabeth (2007). Sacred Mountains and Beloved Fetuses: Can Loving or Worshipping Something Give It Moral Status? *Philosophical Studies* 133(1): 55–81.

Harman, Elizabeth (2011). The Moral Significance of Animal Pain and Animal Death. In T.L. Beauchamp and R.G. Frey (eds.), *The Oxford Handbook of Animal Ethics*. Oxford: Oxford University Press: 726–737.

Hill, Christopher S. (2014). Tim Bayne on the Unity of Consciousness. *Analysis* 74(3): 499–509.

Holtug, Nils (2011). Killing and the Time-relative Interest Account. *Journal of Ethics* 15(3): 169–189.

Hsieh, Nien-hê (2016). Incommensurable Values. In Edward N. Zalta (ed.), *The Stanford Encyclopedia of Philosophy*, Spring 2016 edition, https://plato.stanford.edu/archives/spr2016/entries/value-incommensurable/.

Hutcheson, Francis (1755). *A System of Moral Philosophy*. New York, NY: A.M. Kelley.

Hutcheson, Francis (1769). *An Essay on the Nature and Conduct of the Passions and Affections With Illustrations on the Moral Sense*, 3rd edition. Glasgow: Robert and Andrew Foulis.

James, William (1983). *Talks to Teachers on Psychology and to Students on Some of Life's Ideals*. Cambridge, MA: Harvard University Press.

Jaworska, Agnieszka (2007). Caring and Internality. *Philosophy and Phenomenological Research* 74(3): 529–568.

Jaworska, Agnieszka, and Tannenbaum, Julie (2013). The Grounds of Moral Status. In Edward N. Zalta (ed.), *The Stanford Encyclopedia of Philosophy*, Summer 2013 edition, https://plato.stanford.edu/archives/sum2013/entries/grounds-moral-status/.

Jaworska, Agnieszka, and Tannenbaum, Julie (2014). Person-rearing Relationships as a Key to Higher Moral Status. *Ethics* 124(2): 242–271.

Johnston, Mark (2001). The Authority of Affect. *Philosophy and Phenomenological Research* 63(1): 181–214.

Kahane, Guy, and Savulescu, Julian (2009). Brain Damage and the Moral Significance of Consciousness. *Journal of Medicine and Philosophy* 34(1): 6–26.

Kirchin, S.T. (ed.) (2013). *Thick Concepts*. Oxford: Oxford University Press.

Klein, Colin (2014). The Penumbral Theory of Masochistic Pleasure. *Review of Philosophy and Psychology* 5(1): 41–55.

Korsgaard, Christine M. (1983). Two Distinctions in Goodness. *Philosophical Review* 92(2): 169–195.

Korsgaard, Christine M. (2013). Kantian Ethics, Animals, and the Law. *Oxford Journal of Legal Studies* 33(4): 629–648.

Kriegel, Uriah (2015). *The Varieties of Consciousness*. Oxford: Oxford University Press.

Levy, Neil (2014). The Value of Consciousness. *Journal of Consciousness Studies* 21(1–2): 127–138.

Liao, S. Matthew (2007). Time-Relative Interests and Abortion. *Journal of Moral Philosophy* 4(2): 242–256.

Liao, S. Matthew (2010). The Basis of Human Moral Status. *Journal of Moral Philosophy* 7(2): 159–179.

McCarthy, Cormac (2002). *The Border Trilogy*. London: Picador.

McMahan, Jeff (2002). *The Ethics of Killing: Problems at the Margins of Life*. Oxford: Oxford University Press.

McMahan, Jeff (2015). The Comparative Badness for Animals of Suffering and Death. In Tatjana Višak and Robert Garner (eds.), *The Ethics of Killing Animals*. Oxford: Oxford University Press.

McShane, Katie (2013). Neosentimentalism and the Valence of Attitudes. *Philosophical Studies* 164(3): 747–765.

Mill, John Stuart (1863/2008). *On Liberty and Other Essays*. Oxford: Oxford University Press.

Moller, Dan (2011). Anticipated Emotions and Emotional Valence. *Philosophers' Imprint* 11(9).

Moore, G.E. (1903). *Principia Ethica*. New York: Dover Publications.

Nozick, Robert (1974). *Anarchy, State and Utopia*. New York: Basic Books.

Nozick, Robert (1989). *The Examined Life Philosophical Meditations*. New York: Simon & Schuster.

Osborne, Natalie R., Owen, Adrian M., and Fernández-Espejo, Davinia (2015). The Dissociation Between Command Following and Communication in Disorders of Consciousness: An fMRI Study in Healthy Subjects. *Frontiers in Human Neuroscience* 9. doi:10.3389/fnhum.2015.00493.

Owen, Adrian M., Coleman, Martin R., Boly, Melanie, Davis, Matthew H., Laureys, Steven, Jolles, Dietsje, and Pickard, John D. (2006). Detecting Awareness in the Conscious State. *Science* 313: 1402.

Perrin, Fabien, Castro, Maïté, Tillmann, Barbara, and Luauté, Jacques (2015). Promoting the Use of Personally Relevant Stimuli for Investigating Patients With Disorders of Consciousness. *Frontiers in Psychology* 6: 1102. doi:10.3389/fpsyg.2015.01102.

Pitt, David (2004). The Phenomenology of Cognition, or, What Is It Like to Think that *P*? *Philosophy and Phenomenological Research* 69(1): 1–36.

Plato (1892). *The Dialogues of Plato Translated Into English With Analyses and Introductions by B. Jowett, M.A. in Five Volumes*, trans. Benjamin Jowett, 3rd edition revised and corrected. Oxford: Oxford University Press.

Pochon, Régis, and Declercq, Christelle (2013). Emotion Recognition by Children With Down Syndrome: A Longitudinal Study. *Journal of Intellectual and Developmental Disability* 38(4): 332–343.

Proust, Marcel (1922). *Remembrance of Things Past: Swann's Way*, trans. C.K. Scott Moncrief. London: Chatto and Windus.

Rabinowicz, Wlodek, and Rønnow-Rasmussen, Toni (2000). A Distinction in Value: Intrinsic and for Its Own Sake. *Proceedings of the Aristotelian Society* 100(1): 33–51.

Rachels, James (2004). Drawing Lines. In Cass R. Sunstein and Martha Craven Nussbaum (eds.), *Animal Rights: Current Debates and New Directions*. Oxford: Oxford University Press: 162–174.

Regan, Donald (2004). Why Am I My Brother's Keeper? In R. Jay Wallace, Samuel Scheffler and Michael Smith (eds.), *Reason and Value: Themes From the Philosophy of Joseph Raz*. Oxford: Clarendon Press.

Riley, Jonathan (2008). What Are Millian Qualitative Superiorities? *Prolegomena* 7(1): 61–79.

Riley, Jonathan (2009). Millian Qualitative Superiorities and Utilitarianism, Part II: Jonathan Riley. *Utilitas* 21(2): 127–143.

Rollin, Bernard E. (1981). *Animal Rights and Human Morality*. Amherst, NY: Prometheus Books.

Rønnow-Rasmussen, Toni (2011). *Personal Value*. Oxford: Oxford University Press.

Rosati, Connie S. (2008). Objectivism and Relational Good. *Social Philosophy and Policy* 25(1): 314–349.

Ross, W.D. (1930). *The Right and the Good*. Oxford: Clarendon Press.

Rowlands, Mark (2012). *Can Animals Be Moral*? New York: Oxford University Press.

Russell, Bertrand (1971). *The Autobiography of Bertrand Russell, Volume 1*. London: Allen & Unwin.

Sachs, Benjamin (2011). The Status of Moral Status. *Pacific Philosophical Quarterly* 92(1): 87–104.

Scarantino, Andrea (2014). The Motivational Theory of Emotions. In D'Arms, Justin, and Jacobson, Daniel (eds.). *Moral Psychology and Human Agency: Philosophical Essays on the Science of Ethics*. Oxford: Oxford University Press: 156–185.

Schmidt-Petri, Christoph (2006). On an Interpretation of Mill's Qualitative Utilitarianism. *Prolegomena* 5(2): 165–177.

Schroeter, Laura, Schroeter, François, and Jones, Karen (2015). Do Emotions Represent Values? *Dialectica* 69(3): 357–380.

Sebo, Jeff (2017). Agency and Moral Status. *Journal of Moral Philosophy* 14(1): 1–22.

Shepherd, Joshua (2016a). Consciousness and Quality of Life Research. *American Journal of Bioethics: Neuroscience* 7(1): 54–55.

Shepherd, Joshua (2016b). Moral Conflict in the Minimally Conscious State. In Walter Sinnott-Armstrong (ed.), *Finding Consciousness: The Neuroscience, Ethics, and Law of Severe Brain Damage*. Oxford: Oxford University Press: 160–179.

Shepherd, Joshua (2017). The Moral Insignificance of Self-consciousness. *European Journal of Philosophy* 25(1).

Siewert, Charles (1998). *The Significance of Consciousness*. Princeton, NJ: Princeton University Press.

Smuts, Aaron (2009). Art and Negative Affect. *Philosophy Compass* 4(1): 39–55.

Solomon, Robert C. (2003). *Not Passion's Slave: Emotions and Choice*. Oxford: Oxford University Press.

Stevenson, Robert Louis (2004). *Across the Plains*. Fairfield, IA: 1st World Publisher.

Strasser, Mark Philip (1987). Hutcheson on the Higher and Lower Pleasures. *Journal of the History of Philosophy* 25(4): 517–531.

Sumner, L.W. (1992). Welfare, Happiness, and Pleasure. *Utilitas* 4(2): 199.

Sumner, L.W. (1996). *Welfare, Happiness, and Ethics*. Oxford: Oxford University Press.

Tappolet, Christine (2016). *Emotions, Value, and Agency*. Oxford: Oxford University Press.

Todd, Cain (2014). Relatively Fitting Emotions and Apparently Objective Values. In Roeser, Sabine, and Todd, Cain (eds.). *Emotion and Value*. Oxford: Oxford University Press: 90–106.

Tooley, Michael (1972). Abortion and Infanticide. *Philosophy and Public Affairs* 2(1): 37–65.

van Gameren-Oosterom, Helma B.M., Fekkes, Minne, Buitendijk, Simone E., Mohangoo, Ashna D., Bruil, Jeanet, and Van Wouwe, Jacobus P. (2011). Development, Problem Behavior, and Quality of Life in a Population Based Sample of Eight-year-old Children With Down Syndrome. *PLoS ONE* 6(7): e21879.

Van Hof, M.W. (1970). Interocular Transfer in the Rabbit. *Experimental Neurology* 26(1): 103–108.

Varner, Gary E. (2012). *Personhood, Ethics, and Animal Cognition: Situating Animals in Hare's Two Level Utilitarianism*. Oxford: Oxford University Press.

Warren, Mary Anne (1997). *Moral Status: Obligations to Persons and Other Living Things*. Oxford: Clarendon Press.

Weyl, Hermann (1949). *Philosophy of Mathematics and Natural Science*. Princeton, NJ: Princeton University Press.

Wiggins, David (1987). A Sensible Subjectivism? In *Needs, Values, Truth: Essays in the Philosophy of Value*. Oxford: Blackwell.

Zentall, Thomas R., and Wasserman, Edward A. (eds.) (2012). *The Oxford Handbook of Comparative Cognition*. Oxford: Oxford University Press.

Zimmerman, Michael J. (2015). Intrinsic vs. Extrinsic Value. In Edward N. Zalta (ed.), *The Stanford Encyclopedia of Philosophy*, Spring 2015 edition, https://plato.stanford.edu/archives/spr2015/entries/value-intrinsic-extrinsic/.

Index